Scot-free...and then some

Scot-free...and then some

⚘

Memoirs and Meditations

Dorothy Scott Beaman

All scripture references are from The Holy Bible, New King James Version
Copyright 1982 by Thomas Nelson, Inc.

Credit is due to West Dunbartonshire Libraries & Cultural Services
for permission to use material from The Clydebank Blitz book.

Copyright © 2016 Dorothy Scott Beaman
All rights reserved.
ISBN-13: 9781519147059
ISBN-10: 1519147058

Dedication

*I would like to dedicate this book to my wonderful parents,
Tom & Margaret (Ness) Scott*

With great fortitude, wisdom, humor and encouragement, they raised us to believe we could achieve the goals that we set for ourselves.

Acknowledgements

MANY PEOPLE HAVE contributed their time and wisdom to help me with this book. Laura, Marville, MaryLee, and Megan, thank you for your friendship and help with my writing. Readers especially will be grateful for your suggestions! Jeanie Kerner, your knowledge and generosity with your time is so appreciated.

My husband, Bob, has endured long hours alone, while I worked on this. Fortunately, Bob is an amazing artist and makes use of his time with art projects, so we often spend time on our projects together. And our pastor for 26 years, Jess Strickland of Living Hope in Aloha, Oregon, has contributed immensely to our lives.

Above all, grateful thanks to my Lord Jesus Christ, for His salvation and love that drew me to Himself all those years ago, and still guides my life day by day.

Preface

THERE IS CALLIGRAPHY in our elevator that says, "Home is where your story begins." I like that!

This story started with an invitation from four gal friends to join their writing group. "I'd enjoy that," I told them, "but I don't have a clue what I would write about." They said they'd been meeting for a while, and had written their life stories. That sounded like something I could do, so two weeks later I showed up with my life story, about three pages double spaced. In brevity, it resembled Julius Caesar's "I came, I saw, I conquered." After their laughter died down, I got some valuable insight into what they were expecting, and that started one of the most enjoyable hobbies I have had.

How times have changed! In our lifetime, we are experiencing an electronic revolution that rivals or even surpasses the industrial revolution in the 1800s. Within a few miles of our home, we have several huge plants employing tens of thousands of people making all the newest electronic gadgets. The home sewing machines that I grew up with are no longer considered a necessity; who makes their kids' dresses nowadays?

One of my hopes is that this book will inspire readers to contemplate writing their own story, for their family and friends, and for their own enjoyment. Perhaps the meditations will remind you of promises the Lord has given to you, and how they have contributed to your life. Your children and grandchildren will be grateful to have your story written down.

Table of Contents

Acknowledgements · vii
Preface · ix

Chapter 1	The Blitz ·	1
Chapter 2	The Aftermath ·	9
Chapter 3	School years ·	15
Chapter 4	High School ·	25
Chapter 5	Where it All Began ·	31
Chapter 6	Where was God in all of this? · · · · · · · · · · · · · · · ·	39
Chapter 7	The nest is getting empty · · · · · · · · · · · · · · · · · · ·	53
Chapter 8	Day of Departure - July 26, 1957 · · · · · · · · · · · · · ·	59
Chapter 9	Vessel of Change ·	63
Chapter 10	On the High Seas in the 1950s · · · · · · · · · · · · · · ·	69
Chapter 11	Bien Venu au Canada ·	75
Chapter 12	On the Road Again ·	81
Chapter 13	Finding What I Was Looking For · · · · · · · · · · · · · ·	85
Chapter 14	He who Findeth a Wife ·	93

CHAPTER 1

The Blitz

"Wake up, sweetie!" It was Tommy, my 13-year-old brother. "We need to go out to the shelter." In the middle of a dream, what sounded like music changed quickly to the reality of sirens. I could feel the strength of his arms, as he picked me up from my lower bunk, leaving the blanket trailing on the floor. Heaving me over his shoulder, Tommy carried me downstairs, out of the warm house into the chill of our back yard, and down into the air raid shelter. At 3-1/2 years old, it's my earliest memory, and as young as I was, I knew in my sleepyhead mind what the screaming air raid sirens meant. In a few short minutes, horrible planes would be droning overhead, dropping bombs. This was in March 1941.

The sobering announcement that Britain was at war with Nazi Germany was made by Prime Minister Chamberlain from 10 Downing Street, on Sunday September 3, 1939. The tipping point was that Germany had invaded Poland, an ally of Britain. Even before this, school children in Clydebank, Scotland were carrying identity cards and gas masks, and many had already been evacuated to small towns away from the immediate area.

At the start of the war, the country had expected immediate trouble, and three of my older siblings, Isabel (14), Tommy (12), and Betty (9), were evacuated to the village of Blairmore, which was about 35 miles from our home. It was a sleepy seaside place that in normal times drew city residents in search of tranquil vacations. My oldest brother, George (16), and my sister Jessie (5) and I remained at home with our parents.

Since Daddy had to keep his shop open, Mother accompanied Isabel, Tommy and Betty to the largest assembly area in the village, the school hall. The children were lined up in families, and villagers who came selected the children they wanted to take. Most wanted only one or two, so there was no question but that our three had to be split up. Tommy went with a family who had boys, and my two sisters stayed together in another home, with the lofty name of Blairmore House, owned by Mr. & Mrs. Highgate.

Happily, there were a few of their friends from school who were also taken to Blairmore. Unlike some unpleasant stories, these families were wonderful to their new charges. Mother visited every Saturday to bring treats. It was a long journey by train and ferry, accompanied by two straggling preschoolers.

The two families my brother and sisters lived with had children about their same ages, from about 9 to 14. The Highgates had a small rowboat, and Betty remembers going out in the rowboat with five or six of the kids to where British, U.S., and Canadian warships and aircraft carriers were anchored in the River Clyde. We're talking deep water!

Tommy rowed around the ships in the choppy water, until the sailors spotted them and threw them some big red Mackintosh apples. They had great fun picking the apples out of the water! Betty remembers it happening several times, and shudders now, realizing how dangerous it must have been. Of course, there was no thought of life jackets.

The kids were there about nine months, before returning home the following summer. Because of the presumed calm, evacuees began to trickle back to Clydebank and life resumed some form of normalcy. But behind the scenes, preparations continued for what was considered inevitable.

These preparations included air raid shelters, provided to homes that had yards big enough to accommodate them. Called Anderson shelters, they consisted of corrugated steel sheets, curved for greater strength, like miniature Quonset huts; my Dad, with George and Tommy, had sunk ours about three or four feet into the ground in our back yard. About 6 feet by 7 feet, they could be made quite tolerable, if you discounted dampness and lack of facilities.

Clydebank was a known target mainly because of two things: a huge factory, operated by the Singer Sewing Machine Company, and John Brown's Shipyards. Singer's employed more than ten thousand men and women, and had been converted to the manufacture of armaments and ammunition. Thousands of men at John Brown's were already building ships to be used in the war effort. There were also some ordnance factories in the area, as well as other industrial targets. However, the expected air raids didn't come at the beginning of the war. Sirens were activated at least forty times before March 1941, but they were mostly warnings for single planes on reconnaissance. We made many trips to the shelter in case they were for real.

Our home had a brick wall about three feet high across the street side of our property, and on top of that was an ornamental wrought-iron fence. Any rust spots were painted over every year or two with shiny black paint. But steel was a needed commodity for a country at war, so workers came along with blow torches, indiscriminately cutting off the steel where it entered the brick wall. Although nobody liked it, there were few objections as it was all part of the war effort, and the country was united in standing up to the Nazi threat. These same workers also took donations of pots and pans.

Public buildings were sand-bagged and windows blacked out so that no light shone through. ARP (Air Raid Precaution) wardens patrolled the streets looking for homes that were not thoroughly dark. As an ARP warden, Daddy had a huge hand-held wooden rattle with handles that could be turned like a bicycle wheel. They were used by the wardens if they found windows with light showing. The rat-a-tat rattles were so loud, they sounded like steam rollers going along the street.

My sister Jessie and I were put to bed in "siren suits," heavy one-piece sleeper-type garments, so that if sirens sounded we could leave without having to hunt for coats. My parents and older siblings grabbed what coats and blankets they could get their hands on quickly and fled the house. The shelter was my destination that night on my brother's shoulder, with my arms wrapped around his neck. Tommy and I joined the rest of the family in the awful time of waiting, and this time it was not a false alarm.

On Thursday, March 13, 1941, the 9 o'clock BBC radio news from London had just started when the wail of sirens was heard. Soon planes came roaring directly overhead, at a very low altitude. Loud, then faint, and loud again, they sounded like racecars keeping pace around a track as they dropped their bombs. They flew in groups, and would circle the area, returning again and again to continue their awful work.

Explosions were bursting all around us. Some were quite distant, sounding like a giant clearing his throat. Others were so close they startled us like a sudden sneeze, as the earth shuddered and absorbed the blast. My mother swallowed in relief after each explosion. We talked in whispers, as though the enemy was listening at our shelter door. Was this going to be our time?

It was a clear bright night, with a 'bomber's moon' high in the sky. From 9:30 pm until the All Clear sounded at nearly 6:30 the following morning, more than 500 tons of high explosive bombs were dropped on Clydebank from several hundred low-flying aircraft. Within the city limits more than 500 people were killed, but that number more than doubled when the surrounding area was included. When we came out of the shelter, the morning air was stifling, with a combination of smoke, dust and debris from the damaged properties, that continued to burn or collapse.

This was what would later be called The Clydebank Blitz. "The Blitz" became as familiar an expression, and with the same kind of horrific memories, as "9-11" has for us today here in the United States. It became the dividing line between events "before the Blitz" or "after the Blitz."

After that first night, Daddy noticed there was a hole in the roof of our next door neighbors' home, which was similar to ours. The elderly couple who lived there, Mr. and Mrs. McRae, came out of their shelter and wanted to go in and retrieve some belongings before evacuating to a safer location. Daddy warned them that they shouldn't go in, but they did. Sadly the motion they created activated a bomb that had been dropped, and the home was totally obliterated in one horrifying explosion. Mr. McRae was killed in the explosion, and his wife died shortly after. When their house exploded, it rained debris over the neighborhood and all the surrounding homes were severely damaged.

At the time of the Blitz, our shelter had just a simple wooden door that faced the house, but after the bombing, Daddy and the boys later added a sod baffle wall several feet long, and high enough to help protect the door from any blast. At no time would the shelter have protected us from a direct hit, but it did shield us from peripheral damage from surrounding buildings.

One time a year or so later when the sirens started, we were told we didn't have time to get to the shelter, so all of us piled into a tiny coat closet under our staircase, and stayed there until the All Clear sounded. If a building was damaged and any of it survived, under the staircase was the most likely safe place. Very few homes had basements.

As the war proceeded, the shelter became a bit more sophisticated, covered with about a foot of soil, and topped with grass that made it look like an overblown blister in the lawn. It was equipped with a paraffin heater, electric lighting, and food. Rough cots provided spots for Jessie and me. The older kids and Mum spent the nights on low wooden stools, with their backs against a wall.

Daddy spent many nights on ARP duty and my oldest brother George was on bike patrol. During much of the war, we carried bulky gas masks around our necks, and had gas mask drills at school, but never had to use them. There were special gas masks for babies too young for the standard ones. Baby masks were in the form of small "Moses" baskets, with covers that provided some protection. Daddy had to take these baby baskets to some neighbors who had infants.

The bombing lasted for two nights, March 13 and 14, 1941. There were two more nights in early May, when many more bombs fell. For Clydebank that was it, but the sirens and the solid threats that accompanied them lasted for several more years. We spent many nights in the shelter.

Meditations

The following poem was my attempt to describe the Blitz, for a Creative Writing class in college in 1965. We were to write about a significant event in our life, first in prose, then in verse.

A siren sounds awaking all
      from sleep that held no peace
All, that is, except the child
      within whose dreams
           the siren seems as music

A brother comes, and in his arms
      The strength of youth is felt
And as they go from warmth of room
      to cold of night
           the dreams take flight and vanish

The talk in whispers rises, falls
      The roar of planes to match
Loud, then faint, and loud again
      as cars that race
           keeping the pace around a track

All around explosions burst
      Quite distant, but still clear
But some as sudden sneezes come
      and startle all
           because they fall so near

But then it's past and once again
      Sleep comes upon the child
When dawn returns, the parents leave
      the shelter bleak
           and softly speak their thanks to God

Looking back, it makes me pause to think of what was involved. How many nano seconds does it take for a plane traveling at maybe 200 mph to release a bomb a few hundred feet in the air and have it land 30 yards from where we were huddled by candlelight? That hole could have been in our roof, and may have gone undetected until it was too late. Only by God's Hand was our family saved from disaster. I don't spend a lot of time pondering on those days in my childhood. But from time to time I do give thanks for how He protected us.

Psalm 57:1
Be merciful to me, O God,
be merciful to me!
For my soul trusts in You;
And in the shadow of Your wings
I will make my refuge,
Until these calamities have passed by.

Psalm 44:7-8
But You have saved us from our enemies,
And have put to shame those who hated us.
In God we boast all day long,
And praise Your name forever.

CHAPTER 2

The Aftermath

When we came out of the shelter after the first night, my mother assigned my older siblings jobs to try to get things back to normal. The house was pretty much in shambles, windows mostly broken and the red sandstone walls were pock-marked with shrapnel. The boys swept up the glass and debris outside and helped some neighbors, while Isabel, (the second of the six kids) was given the task of sweeping all the plaster that had fallen from the ceilings inside.

Even when bombs fell a block or two away, the reverberation was felt in our home. The ceilings were a lath-and-plaster type of construction, and there wasn't much plaster left. So Isabel worked hard with a broom and had gathered up all she could find on the ground floor.

In the middle of the horrors of the Blitz, there are some things that, in retrospect, are quite comical. Isabel had just finished sweeping when the house next door blew up. Pictures were knocked off the walls and broken, and whatever plaster was left on the ceilings ended up on the floor. She had to start all over again, this time with plaster sprinkled throughout her hair! She wasn't a happy camper!

That wasn't the only place the plaster fell. Over the years, Mum had made lots of jam and marmalade. The jam always set without a problem, but she was never able to get marmalade to set—until that night! She had left a huge pot of beautifully set marmalade uncovered on the stove, waiting to be put into jars in the morning. And yes, in the morning it too was covered with plaster.

Another funny story, as it is told in the book about the Blitz* that my high school history teacher wrote, is about a family that was rushing to their shelter. Suddenly, the father turned and headed back toward their house.

"Where are you goin'?" asked his son.

"Back for m' teeth," was the response.

"Don't be daft! It's not pies they're droppin'!"

After the first night of bombs, ARP wardens told us to meet down at the Regal Cinema on Dumbarton Road, where shuttle buses would take us out of town to safety. The plan was to take refugees down to the Vale of Leven, near Loch Lomond. However, while Mum and all of us children were waiting to be picked up at the cinema, the sirens started again, and we were now in an even more dangerous location, very close to the shipyards which were the primary target.

John Brown's shipyard itself received less damage than one would have thought, possibly because of a Polish destroyer which happened to be in dry dock there for repairs. During the first night, the Polish crews emptied their magazines with a terrific barrage of Ack-Ack guns, and they may have been responsible for bringing down at least one German plane.

There was a big Union Church nearby, and some of the men kicked in the door; we spent the second night in the hall of that church. Mum stayed awake all night, sitting on the floor with her back against the platform wall, singing hymns as the bombs dropped around the area. At times I was in Mum's lap, and sometimes I snuggled next to my big sister on the wooden floor. Adding to the distress, the guns on the Polish ship went off throughout the night whenever there were planes circling. Daddy thought we were safely out of town, and was horrified when we showed up at home the next day.

It wasn't a simple stroll home, either. The town was smothered in black smoke and dust. The streets were cluttered with debris from bombed out buildings, and in many cases walls several stories high were threatening to collapse, or had already collapsed, blocking passage completely.

Along the main streets, there were hundreds of tenements three or four stories high. They had been built around the turn of the century to accommodate workers who had come for the industrial expansion that was happening in the area. They were prime targets for the planes, and a single bomb could easily devastate a whole block of homes. Rooms full of broken furniture were exposed to the world, much of it burning from fires exploding into the rooms from fireplaces that had once spread comforting heat.

We had to pick our way through this, climb over mountains of rubble, step by careful step, an exhausted mother, two preschoolers and three of the older children. It was about a mile from the church back home. The roads throughout the whole town were mostly blocked to traffic such as ambulances and fire trucks, and bike messengers were the only dependable means of getting news around. There were numerous accounts of heroism by ambulance, police and fire personnel, many of whom were later awarded medals for their bravery. Out of 12,000 homes, only seven in the whole town were left intact, and around 40,000 people were left homeless.

After the second night, shuttle services transported hundreds of residents (including Mum and five of us kids) across the River Clyde to Johnstone, not as far as Blairmore but still much safer than our town. Because Mum insisted that we all stay together, housing options were few. This resulted in our living for several months with a wealthy family. We didn't actually *live* with them. Although they had several bedrooms, we were given their glass conservatory where they kept their exotic plants! We had few bathroom facilities and used a toilet off their kitchen.

Dad and George continued their patrols and visited when they could. I can't remember how mother handled the cooking or other chores or errands. It probably wasn't very comfortable for the family that housed us either. After all, there we were, six strangers sharing their property, including four young sisters and Tommy, who was very prone to get into mischief!

While staying at this home, there is one game we played that later became the subject of family dinner-time teasing. It was when we were playing soldiers in some kind of army. In the grounds, they had a lovely pool, and around it were paved pathways. One of the young sons of the home was the self-designated sergeant, and paid us each a penny a week for being in his army! It was big stuff to us, because you could get candy for a penny, or pay a bus fare. He shouted out orders like "Left TURN,

Right TURN" and we were to follow his instructions. Well, we heard a splash, and looked around to see 5-year-old Jessie standing up to her waist in the pond, soaked to the skin, with water dripping off her head. Her little dress was sticking to her body like so much plastic wrap.

"What happened to you?" we all asked.

"Well, he didn't say Right TURN, so I kept on going!"

At the time of the blitz, my brother George had been a bike messenger for the town. Later he joined the Royal Navy. Just three years after the blitz, almost to the day, George was killed when his plane went down in the Indian Ocean—the price one family had to pay for freedom. I remember being behind my mother's skirt when she went to the front door to get the yellow telegram from the messenger. The first words were "We regret to inform you…" George had just turned 20, a pilot in the Fleet Air Arm, which was the air branch of the Royal Navy, and he flew off the aircraft carrier HMS Illustrious. There had been a number of accidents with the plane he was flying, including veteran pilots, and the Navy took that type of plane out of service after George's death.

The impact the news had on my parents and older siblings was indescribable. As our family stumbled through the days and weeks following, something was made clearer to me than could have been by any other means. My parents' love for their firstborn son was vast and unlimited. Of course, it changed our family forever. George is remembered as a quiet, serious and wholly dependable young man.

I would like to have more memories of George, but because his leaves were scarce during the war, he was seldom able to come home. One of the few memories I have is sitting in his lap, with my head against his chest, and for the first time I heard a heart beating in my ear. It may have been his last leave. I was about six years old, and I know he was very fond of his two wee sisters.

George was never found, and that marked my life in an odd way for a year or two. I kept thinking, well maybe—just maybe—they'll find him and he'll come home. When the front doorbell would ring, I'd listen carefully in case it was George. Of course, it was not to be.

For several years, a young man, Harry Leigh, who had flown with George and was usually his "observer" on the plane, kept in touch with our family. He was a great comfort to our parents, and was the one who brought George's belongings home after his death. Harry never forgot Jessie's and my birthdays; and for several years he sent us books and gifts at Christmas. I well remember "Veronica at the Wells," a story I read several times about a young girl at Sadler Wells Ballet in London. Harry was fortunate not to have been on that ill-fated flight. Dad and Mum became very fond of him and I believe they were guests at his wedding in Coventry, England a few years later.

Although the sirens continued many times after that spring, for Clydebank and the surrounding area there were no more nights of bombing. In the summer of 1945 we were visiting near Blairmore when the end of the war was announced. All of us—residents, visitors and whoever happened to be in town—walked around the Holy Loch in one huge glorious party-cum-parade.

The U.S. and Canadian ships, along with several British warships that were anchored in the Firth of Clyde and the Holy Loch, joined in the celebration by tooting their ships' loud horns. There was lots of singing; and I remember singing "Don't Fence Me In," as we skipped along! That was an exhilarating evening. Strangers joked and hugged each other like brothers. Everyone was giddy with overwhelming relief and joy that this horrendous war was over.

A couple of years later, Daddy and Tommy broke down the shelter and leveled the back yard to its former condition. However, several of our neighbors kept their shelters intact and used them to store yard tools etc. Some were made quite attractive, with decorative rock and plants, but I was glad Daddy wanted ours gone. It held too many memories.

* The Clydebank Blitz, by I. M. M. MacPhail
Clydebank Town Council 1974

Meditations

George's death was a huge blow to my parents. But it will always be a testament to me of their steadfastness in the face of overwhelming disaster. My grandfather, who had been living with us for some time because of his ill health, passed away shortly after George; yet my mother was able to be strong for the family in spite of her immense grief. God never gives us more than we can handle with His magnificent grace.

Psalm 32:7
You are my hiding place;
You shall preserve me from trouble;
You shall surround me with songs of deliverance.

Psalm 34:18
The Lord is near to those who have a broken heart, and saves such as have a contrite spirit.

Isaiah 43:2
When you pass through the waters, I will be with you; And through the rivers, they shall not overflow you. When you walk through the fire, you shall not be burned, nor shall the flame scorch you.

For more information about the Blitz, there are many articles and photographs on line. Google "Clydebank Blitz"

CHAPTER 3

School years

After the war, the "debris" (a word that became a part of our vocabulary, sans the French accent) where the house next door had been bombed, became somewhat of a play area for us. For a couple of years, a huge oak tree that still stands today next to the neighbors' lot, told its own story, with clothes, sheets and lacy curtains rotting in its branches. The debris became the place for yard clippings, and was the location of our annual bonfire in the fall to celebrate Guy Fawkes Day. He tried to blow up the Houses of Parliament some time back in the 1600s! That was our occasion for not-very-sophisticated fireworks. There was a ditty that we sang, "Remember, Remember, the fifth of November—Gunpowder, treason, and plots."

I had a little friend, Ruby Wright, whose daddy was an evangelist. She lived on Stevenson Street and we played together a lot. After the war, German prisoners of war were brought in to rebuild neighborhoods that had been totally destroyed, so we often had huge lorries filled with POWs drive past our home. Ruby would wave at them, and they would wave back. But I refused to wave. In my eight-year-old mind, they were still the enemy. Ruby told me I should forgive them, like Jesus had forgiven us. It was probably my first Gospel message, but I still wouldn't wave!

Along with several western countries, Britain participated in daylight savings time, in order to make the most of the daylight hours. However, during the war years, clocks were adjusted two hours ahead of standard time, to what was known as Double Summer Time. It was done to conserve fuel, and allow people working in the munitions industries to get home before blackout.

Because of this, we had daylight well past our normal bedtime. The only time I remember a spanking from Daddy was the result of this. I was playing out in the back yard, and he had called me in several times for bed. I was having too much fun! So when I did go in, he put me over his knee and swatted me with his rolled up newspaper. Didn't hurt my bottom much, but my feelings got hurt! My usual punishment was being stood in the corner for a few minutes, and it usually happened during meals. Again, it didn't hurt me, but I shed plenty of tears that ran down the wall and puddled on the linoleum floor.

Around the end of the war, when the shipping channels were safe, we received the first of several "care" boxes from an aunt and uncle in Atlanta, Georgia. What a treat those were! The first one contained beautiful dolls for Jessie and me. They had soft skin and eyes that closed, and we named them after my aunt and cousin, May and Sandra. Mum knitted numerous outfits for them, and we played with them for years. The only other contents I remember were packets of Jello which we had never seen before, and loads of candy, which they used to pad the empty corners. We didn't particularly care for the American candy!

Dalmuir Primary School was a three-story classic-style red sandstone building not far from our home. My memories from those years are a jumbled assortment of friends, activities, Brownies, "rounders" (our version of baseball that we played in the street), and family events. For some time we had a sewing bee led by a neighbor in their glassed-in porch.

One comical thing I remember is a "class" we had in very early grades. Miss McDonald came into the room carrying a cardboard box filled with old (clean) rags. She proceeded to give us an illustration of how we should blow our nose! Then she passed around the rags, and showed us how to close one nostril and blow, then change to the other nostril and blow! I'm thinking there must have been a lot of runny noses in class, because I'm sure that wasn't in the curriculum!

One of my early memories involving my siblings is of Isabel. Towards the end of the war, Isabel served with the NAAFI—the Navy, Army, and Air Force Institutes. The NAAFI somewhat filled the role of the USO, although it was a government agency. They had military uniforms, ran thousands of canteens, organized entertainment for the troops, and served both at home and overseas wherever troops were serving, including on board ships. The NAAFI is still operating today.

When Jessie and I were little tykes, we always looked forward to when Isabel was home on leave. At bedtime, she would come upstairs and, sitting on the windowsill, she would weave the most wonderful stories for us, built around three make-believe characters, Hen Chung, Chicken Chung, and Charlie Percy. I have no idea what the stories were about, but their names will be forever etched on my memory! Her imagination kept us enthralled as she made up plots as she went along.

I must have been a sleep-walker, because I remember waking up sitting on that same windowsill. Mum and Daddy were standing by me, with Betty and Jessie looking on. Apparently I had made my way from the bed to the windowsill before Betty went and told my folks about it. I don't remember how they woke me up. It could have been a bit scary for Jessie and Betty, because our window was always kept open overnight, unless it was foggy outside.

When we were about eight or nine, we had to learn to use a sewing machine. Mum had one at home, but hers was a small portable Singer (of course—you had to support the local economy). She turned the wheel with her right hand while guiding the material with the other. The ones at school were monsters, with treadles which were torment for little girls with weak little ankles that refused to keep the treadle moving evenly. We also learned how to knit, and I went home with a perfectly beautiful pair of socks, knitted with four needles, complete with a "turned heel." Of course it didn't diminish my pride that the socks were so tight I could hardly get them over my big toe.

Talking about toes, one time in grade school I was summoned to the Head Master's office, for what I didn't have a clue. However, it was nothing I had done wrong. Instead, it was something that I had—BIG FEET! Because I was tall for my age, my feet were measured and I was given extra shoe coupons, which of course delighted my parents. Maybe we got them because when we were outgrowing our shoes, Mum would take a razor and cut the leather off the end so our toes could peek through, making do-it-yourself sandals. We thought they were A-Okay and didn't give it a thought. I know we weren't the only family that did that.

When I was about nine or ten, when school was out one summer I was bored and moped around, asking Mum what I could do. "Why don't you pick some flowers and go over and put them on Granny Ness's grave?" was her suggestion. I must have been REALLY bored, because it sounded like a good idea! I went out to the garden and picked a bunch of flowers and headed out. It was about a mile walk to the cemetery.

Along the last stretch of road leading to the cemetery, there were several smart-aleck boys playing in the street, kicking a football around. I skirted them, and kept going. However, after hunting for quite a while in the cemetery, I realized I had no idea where the grave was, and gave up looking. Heading back along Montrose Street, I was still clutching the now pretty limp flowers. The same boys were still there, but now their attention wasn't on the ball but on me. One of them yelled at me, "What's the matter, hen? Was yer granny no' hame?" My mother got a laugh out of it, and asked me why on earth I didn't leave them on someone else's grave!

Even after the war was over in 1945, families experienced rationing of most everyday things, including eggs (one egg per person a week), bread, clothing, shoes, and sugar. I distinctly remember the BU's ("bread units"), maybe because the sound kind of ran together. However, with six now in our family and each one entitled to a ration book, we kids never felt threatened with hunger. Daddy and Tommy tilled up our front lawn and planted rows of potatoes that supplied us well.

About this same time, I remember Mum coming home from town with a banana. It was something we had never seen before, and we gazed in wonder as she peeled it and doled out little rounds to all of us. One day Daddy had a queue outside the shop when the word got around "Galbraith's has bananas! Galbraith's has bananas!" Betty, who by that time was working with Daddy in the shop, said the people standing in line scattered quickly to the grocery store a few doors down to snag some of that almost forgotten fruit.

All during my growing up years, my father was a shopkeeper—a "newsagent and tobacconist" to be exact. It was also the local hardware, newspaper, toy, and sundry shop. He sold household goods like whitening that housewives would buy to whiten the steps at their front door. Jessie and I enjoyed going down to the shop, where we would try to roll pennies for the bank, and there was a bakery nearby that sold wonderful rolls!

But the main source of income was tobacco products, and when Singers' employees got paid on Fridays, there would be a long queue out the door. When Daddy was getting an overly large number of unsaleable things, he would put up a sign that said "Cigarettes for customers only." So if you bought a comb or a pencil for a few pennies you were "a customer," and Daddy got his leftovers cleared out!

Because of the newspaper factor, Daddy seldom got a day off. But two years after the war ended, he left the shop with a dependable assistant, and he and Mum took Betty, Jessie and me off to St. Andrews for a week. It was his home town, and has always been a favorite of our family. We stayed in The Station & Windsor Hotel. One of the most fascinating features of the hotel was that if you left your dirty shoes outside your door, some genie would come around during the night and clean them. So of course we did this with abandon!

I haven't mentioned this before, but my father was a veteran of World War I (what we called The Great War.) He had lost a leg, and had a wooden leg. And it WAS wood. He used thumb tacks to keep his sock up!! Daddy had a great sense of humor and would sometimes tease us by having us slap his leg, and we always got caught hitting the wrong leg!

Well, at the St. Andrews hotel, at bedtime Betty, Jessie and I would take off our shoes, and set them at the door. Daddy also put his one regular shoe out for cleaning, but his was always left untouched. After two or three tries, he decided he'd had enough. He finally put both shoes out—one of them with a leg attached! The next morning, they were both cleaned. (To be honest, I don't personally remember this event, but it became such a legend in our family, it either happened or it didn't...)

When I was about ten years old, our family was planning a vacation trip to the south of England. It was the last day of school, and everyone was pretty excited. But I came home from school that day not feeling well. As was the custom when the doctor was called, I was put in Mum and Daddy's room, a pathetic little slip of a girl in a massive grown-up bed. Dr. Crombie came in and very quickly assessed the problem. I had scarlet fever.

An ambulance came and drove me to Blawarthill Hospital about five miles away, and I was given a bed in a large ward with about 10 or 12 other boys and girls. The aging hospital was probably at least 75 years old, and our ward was a separate building, single level, kind of like a barracks. Across a large lawn there was another similar building that we were told had TB patients, quarantined of course.

We were also in quarantine the whole time, and not allowed any visitors at all. Like most families, we didn't have a car so when they could get away, Mum and Daddy would come up by bus. I could see them as they approached the door and then they'd be out of sight until they left. They soon learned where my bed was and they would come up to the window, shading their eyes with their hand as they peered through, looking for me. We waved at each other as they came and left. I knew when they left there would be surprises for me. Daddy's shop sold toys, books and trinkets that were treasures to a child, and I think he cleaned out shop each time they came. I can hardly imagine the pain it must have been for them, to leave their little girl in hospital without even getting in to hug her.

Part of our entertainment in the ward happened at night after our evening meal. We knew there were little mice scampering around, and I soon learned from the other kids to keep some crumbs from my meals so I could feed them! After things quieted down in the evening and the staff left, we'd drop the crumbs we had been saving and wait. Sure enough in a couple of minutes here would come one mouse, then another, and our heads would hang over the edge of our beds watching them eat. It was great fun! The nurses would have been horrified if they had known what we were doing!

After three weeks, I was told I'd be going home. But just before the last day I was up helping the nurse make my bed, straightening the sheet. I cried "Ouch!" Big mistake. She asked me what was the matter and I told her I had a crick in my wrist. That was the end of my going home. They were afraid I might be getting rheumatic fever and kept me for another three weeks. Six weeks total. So much for vacation time. But we did go the following year.

My hospital stay helped solve one of the fusses that Jessie and I had. Jessie had an eye problem, and has worn glasses all her life. When she was 11, she was able to go into hospital in Glasgow for an operation, and came home with perfectly straight eyes. But during her hospital stay, she had learned how to make her bed the way the nurses did. So when she came home, she was very fussy about the corners of our bed being done like an envelope. I just wanted to straighten things up and get on with life. After I got home from my hospital experience, I too had learned how to correctly make the bed and it made for a more peaceful chore!

Daddy had one favorite hobby, and that was stamp collecting. I can still see him poring over his albums, with a magnifying glass in his hand. He had a little dish with water in it, and with tweezers he would soak old envelope paper off the back of the stamps. Then when they were dry, he'd glue tiny paper "hinges" on the back of the stamps, and each stamp would find a very particular space in one of his many stamp albums.

We had what we called a tallboy in our kitchen, with about six drawers. One of the drawers had linens, table cloths, tea towels, and such things, and most importantly, Daddy's linen table napkin, carefully rolled into a napkin ring. If we sat down to dinner and his napkin wasn't on his plate, all he would have to say was "Who set the table?" and one of us would scamper over to get his napkin. It was kind of a favorite little tradition at dinner time, the kind of thing that made our house a home.

There were two lower drawers whose use escapes me now. BUT the bottom drawer—ah that was strictly off limits to us, because it was where

Daddy kept his stamp collection. Because we adored our parents, I guess it was natural that we wanted to collect stamps also. So when we were still in primary school, Jessie and I had our own stamp collections, made up of duplicates that took our fancy, and colorful stamps of no value. Our little grade school fingers had a time with those hinges! They seemed to get stuck every place except where we wanted them.

I remember sitting at the kitchen table, looking through an atlas to find where Sierra Leone or Tanganyika or Helvetia were. I hunted for Helvetia for a while before Daddy realized what I was looking for and taught me that stamps that said Helvetia were from Switzerland. We learned a lot of world geography from our stamp collections.

Meditations

Many homes in Scotland have names, and the name is often used instead of "home." Some of our neighbors' homes were Springfield and Craigforth, sometimes tied to places that had special memories. Isabel's home in the West Highlands was Lecknabaan. Our home was called Glenfender; the name was on our gate when my parents moved there in 1931, and all of us still use Glenfender, in referring to the "old home place." It was not unusual for us to get mail addressed to the Scotts, "Glenfender," Dalmuir, near Glasgow. Dalmuir was an unincorporated area that later became part of Clydebank. The postman knew all the house names.

Glenfender always had lots of activity, with kids of varying ages dashing in and out throughout the day. What we called the kitchen was what now would be called the family room, and it really was a family room for us. There was a coal fireplace, and because it was our only source of heat, we mostly did everything there. It definitely promoted family togetherness! The heat from the fire rose through the chimney and warmed the hot water tank in the only bathroom. Even in summer time, if you wanted a bath, there had to be a fire going. The cooking was done in our "scullery" and the staple every night was a huge pot of potatoes, along with whatever protein Mum could buy. Although we never knew it, money was pretty scarce, but God always provided for our family of six.

Psalm 128:3-4
Your wife shall be like a fruitful vine in the very heart of your house,
Your children like olive plants all around your table. Behold, thus shall the man be blessed who fears the LORD.

Psalm 127:3-5
Behold, children are a heritage from the LORD,
The fruit of the womb is a reward.
Like arrows in the hand of a warrior,
So are the children of one's youth.
Happy is the man who has his quiver full of them.

CHAPTER 4

High School

IN THE SCOTTISH school system at that time, we started high school at the age of eleven or twelve. So as a green 11-year-old I showed up for Miss Gordon's Latin class. We later called her The Gorgon as her classes included some Greek mythology. The Gorgon was a monstrous vicious female creature with sharp fangs whose appearance would turn anyone who laid eyes on it to stone! Miss Gordon's stern mien made sure there was no monkey business in her class.

That first day, as Miss Gordon scanned the roster, her face lit up and she almost glowed as she announced, "Now here's a wonderful Latin name! Who is Dorothy Scott?" I trembled and raised my hand, wondering what was coming next.

"Do you know what your name means?" she asked.

"Yes," I mumbled shyly. "It means Gift of God."

I'm sure she was astonished that I knew. This was long before most anyone talked about what their name meant, but my folks had made sure I knew. It was just one of the unspoken ways my parents showed their love. Another way I knew was when I heard mum tell someone that, when I was delivered by the doctor in their bedroom, the radio was playing "I've got my love to keep me warm!" and she stood with her arm around my waist and drew me close.

One of our teachers, Mrs. O'Hare, was marked forever in our minds because she had what we thought was blue hair. Probably a botched dye job! One day, Mrs. O'Hare, who had a small farm and boarded prize dogs in her kennels, told us she had a dog that needed a home. The trick was you had to have a note from your parents saying you could adopt the dog. Well, I passed the exciting news to my parents who promptly wrote a note. After all, what chance did I have with thirty children in the class? It turned out I was the only one who got a note, so we acquired Sheila, a wonderful dog who was part of our family for the next 13 years. She was a mix between a labrador and a standard-sized French poodle, medium size with black wavy hair. We all loved her!

One day, after we'd had Sheila for a couple of years, I came home from school for lunch. As I opened the gate and started to walk up the path, Sheila came out very gingerly from behind the wooden storm doors at the front door. As I got closer, I realized she was in serious pain. She was completely split from the top of her back right around and exposing her belly, apparently the result of a run-in with a car. This was no ordinary dog—she was our Sheila, and my folks rallied to get her the best care they could find. A lady vet came and picked her up to take her in for treatment.

I was in such a state that I didn't go back to school that afternoon, and Mum wrote a note for my absence. We didn't know if Sheila would be back or not, but a couple of days later she was back home with some huge stitches in her belly and flank. We had to slather ugly white ointment on her wound for weeks, until it gradually closed up. The poor dog looked so awful Mum cut up a towel that we put over her back and tied with tape and string under her tummy. We didn't want people to see her huge wound. Sheila not only recovered, but I believe that was her only trip to the vet, and she lived for another ten years, long after I had left home.

In 1952, our beloved King, George VI, passed away and his oldest daughter became Queen Elizabeth II. Although everyone liked her, Scottish people were very unhappy with the II after her name. The first Queen Elizabeth had been queen of England but not of Scotland. There were quite a few incidents of destruction, bombs blowing up post offices and other places where the II appeared, but eventually people got used to the idea, and the trouble died down.

When the Coronation was approaching in June a year later, there was a great deal of excitement surrounding the event. My parents had not yet acquired a television set, but in order to view the Coronation, they purchased one and placed it in our front room. It had one button, On/Off, and one BBC channel. The livingroom was mostly an unused parlor that had been the boys' bedroom. It was unheated, but that was not a problem at the time of the Coronation; TVs were still a novelty, and Glenfender became the neighborhood viewing place. The house was packed with friends and neighbors as we watched the beautiful young queen being crowned.

About this time, I remember telling Mum that I could never keep straight when our parents' birthdays were. One was July 15, and the other July 18, and I always had to ask which was which. "Oh, that's easy," Mum said. "Your Dad always comes first in this household." That settled it, and I never had to ask again. That was typical of how they treated each other. There was total respect both ways, and if they had disagreements of any kind, they were settled privately between themselves. I don't remember them speaking a cross word to each other.

For some time during my high school years, probably because of having Sheila in our home, I thought it would be great to become a veterinarian. I suppose lots of kids have that idea during their early years! However, during high school it became evident very quickly that my abilities in science would not allow that career path! One term I got a score of 28% in Science!

Most of the time, I came in quite high in rankings in our class, usually third, fourth or fifth. However, my 28% sank those rankings that term, and I was 21st instead! I had to take my report card home to have my parent sign it. Up to that point Daddy had always signed them, but because of the state of that report, I brought it home at lunch time and asked Mum to sign it. A week or so later, Daddy mentioned the fact that he had not seen my report card. "Oh, I had Mum sign it," I responded casually. I don't know if he could read my mind, or if Mum had said something to him, but he told me he wanted to see it. I had to go to the school office and request my card back, and so the awful truth about my science skills, or lack thereof, was found out.

The summer before my senior year, I went to work for Mrs. O'Hare on her farm, feeding piglets and letting individual dogs out to the run. I guess I got in too much of a hurry and during a kennel change, I let a dog out without properly securing the lock of the dog I had just let run. So two of those prize dogs got in a dog fight. I didn't know any better, and thinking the dogs were going to harm each other, I got in the middle trying to stop the fight. Of course I was bitten in several places, on my thighs and hands mainly. So much for my first job. It meant a tetanus shot and torn pants, and lasted only two weeks! But I enjoy telling people that my first job was feeding pigs!

A sorry occasion worth noting in high school was the result of another care package from my aunt and uncle, which had continued coming for many years. This one included chewing gum—a rare and highly desirable treat for us. I took several sticks of gum to school and handed them out at random just before French class one day.

Halfway through class, our teacher Mr. Gray (who lived in Craigforth, the big manor house on the other side of the debris) had had enough. He halted the lesson and told everyone who was chewing to come up to the front. He lined us up, had us dispose of the gum, and proceeded to strap us with his leather strap, double handed, which of course doubled the pain for us. I quickly went from Miss Popular to The Blameworthy One.

After three years of high school, the majority of kids left school, having reached the leaving age of 15. However, Jessie (who was a year ahead of me) and I stayed for two more years. For those two years, we were able to choose a major, like in college. I was good in two areas, and it was difficult to choose between art and music. I had taken piano lessons for several years, and figured I could get decent marks without working too much! So I opted for music. Although I never used it professionally, it gave me a thorough appreciation for classical music, and to this day I still enjoy all kinds of choral and orchestral music.

Daddy (who couldn't carry a tune in a bucket) would have preferred that I take art, and I never really understood why. However I later found that art majors could develop skills in drafting and building design, which would have been an excellent career path. I'm sure that was why Daddy was interested in that route.

In the spring of my senior year, it was announced that there was going to be a ten-day-long trip to Paris for French students who wished to go. It would cost twenty pounds. That evening I pled my case with Mum and Daddy, realizing it was a huge amount of money. (A few months after this my first pay check was three pounds a week.)

After talking it over between themselves, a couple of days later they told me I could go. However, the previous year Jessie had been presented with the same chance and had been turned down. So, ever the equal-opportunity parents, they gave Jessie twenty pounds that she could use for a vacation. So that summer she and her friend Emma spent a week at a holiday resort in England.

The Paris trip was a blast. We traveled by train and ferry, stayed at a boys high school (which was out for vacation), and visited all the important sites in and around Paris. We also had some free time, and one evening back at the dorm, the same Mr. Gray (remember the gum chewing incident?) who was one of our chaperones, got some of us together to give us advice. It was quite improper, he sternly warned us, for young ladies to walk along the streets of Paris smoking! That was all he had to say, and that was the end of our smoking!

I do remember one sad thing that I had never experienced before, and that was homelessness. Where we came from, everybody had somewhere to go at night. But in Paris, there were people sleeping on the streets, usually above vents in the sidewalks that emitted some warm air. I tried to communicate some kind questions to a very old lady and offered her some candy. At first she totally ignored me, but eventually she just reared up and growled like an angry dog. I was half a block away in a flash!

Meditations

My parents named me after a friend whom they had known when they were newlyweds. I didn't particularly like my name as a young person; but as I grew to know the Lord, it was comforting to know that they considered me a gift from God.

I have always been grateful for the way our parents raised us. Now as I look back, I see the correlation between my Father in Heaven and my earthly Daddy. Both could be stern, but it was always for our good. And both my parents had a wonderful sense of humor. I have to believe that our Heavenly "Daddy" has a sense of humor, even if we may have to go through a hard lesson to find it. Actually, all you have to do is look through a picture book of the bird and animal kingdom, and you can see humor everywhere!

Isaiah 45:4-5
I have even called you by your name;
I have named you, though you have not known Me.
I am the LORD, and there is no other;
I will gird you, though you have not known Me.

Psalm 119:9
How can a young man cleanse his way?
By taking heed according to Your word.

CHAPTER 5

Where it All Began

> "Remember the days of old, Consider the years of many generations. Ask your father, and he will show you; your elders, and they will tell you."
>
> — DEUTERONOMY 32:7

As kids, we all felt like we had the best Mum and Daddy in the world. There wasn't a whole lot of discipline, but it was because there were rules in place that we understood and seldom challenged. With six kids, you need rules! Daddy's word was law and we knew better than to disrespect him.

At bedtime every evening, we lined up by his armchair for goodnight kisses. I remember feeling his rough whiskers at the end of the day, but the hug and kiss and the pat on the rear were worth the rub! Then we'd scamper up the 18 stairs to our room, sometimes on all fours, or we'd take them two by two or even three by three. Eighteen fitted several multiplication tables.

Daddy was born in the Kingdom (County) of Fife, on Scotland's east coast, in a farming community outside St. Andrews, the home of golf. The year was 1890, and he was the youngest of eight children. His father, who was a stone mason, died when Daddy was four years old. His next oldest sibling was Jennie, who was 13 years older, and the youngest of three girls.

The other brothers were all older than she, and in the spirit of the times were anxious to explore life in other parts. Around 1900, several of the boys decided they were going to emigrate, and this brought a hard decision for their widowed mother. So at 23 years old, Aunt Jennie moved with Daddy into St. Andrews, while his mother (whose maiden name was also Scott) joined the older boys (and one of their fiancées) headed to America.

Aunt Jennie raised him from the time he was ten until he finished high school and had two years of apprenticeship with an architectural firm. Then in 1908 both of them sailed to Boston, Massachusetts, where several of the brothers had established homes. Because of her unselfish care for him, Daddy and Aunt Jennie had a very close, loving relationship that lasted throughout their lives. It is not exaggerating to say that they adored each other.

Aunt Jennie had a beau in Scotland, who had been a boarder in the family home, no doubt to supplement the family finances. He was also extremely kind, and waited for her until she was ready to set her young charge free. They married, and lived in Montreal, Canada where he was the Head Master of a private boys' academy. After retiring they returned to Scotland. Their story deserves a book by itself.

Because of the difference in ages, Aunt Jennie and Uncle David became like grandparents to us. We loved visiting their beautiful home in Edinburgh, a red sandstone row house with a beautiful white curved staircase. Halfway up the stairs, there was a landing with a small room off of it, which was the "maid's quarters." I don't remember them having a maid, but I remember telling my folks I could be their maid!

In the meantime (back to the story) Daddy was hired by Lockwood Greene & Company, an engineering and construction firm in Boston. They must have seen promise in the young Scotsman, because Daddy quickly rose in the company. He became their point man when they were opening offices along the eastern seaboard and Daddy moved to Spartanburg, South Carolina, Charlotte and Atlanta.

While he was working in these positions, the political situation in Europe was changing quickly and becoming more and more threatening, eventually bringing on World War I. The United States had not entered the war, but Canada had. Daddy had such strong feelings about what was happening in Europe, he opted to go to Canada and enlist in the Canadian Army. He was 24 at the time. (Recently I was able to view his enlistment papers, including his signature, on an ancestry web-site.)

As part of the Canadian Expeditionary Forces, Daddy went to Europe and while there, he was involved in the Battle of the Somme, a lengthy battle that took place in France in 1916. It is recorded as one of the bloodiest battles in history, with over a million casualties, probably exacerbated by the primitive medical facilities in the field. One of the casualties was Daddy, who had to have his lower left leg amputated just above the ankle. Shipped back to Canada, he was hospitalized in Kingston, Ontario, where his unit was stationed. After recuperation, he returned to the States and resumed his career with Lockwood Greene in Atlanta.

While all this was happening, back in Clydebank, in the west of Scotland, a young girl was being raised by her parents who had a newspaper and hardware shop. She was known as a sprightly young woman, not afraid to take risks, maybe because she came between two adventurous brothers. She kept pestering her parents about wanting to emigrate, but they would never agree. Never, that was, until a girlfriend was making plans to go to Canada with her family. At 20 years old, Mum begged her parents to let her go with them and, tired of her pleading, they agreed, since she would be under the watchful eye of the other parents.

When they landed in Canada in 1920, her friend's parents kept her in tow for a short time and after that were out of the picture. So much for guardianship! (Mum said they didn't see each other after they got off the ship, but I find that hard to believe.) Resourceful as she was, she hired on as a governess for a wealthy family who had a toddler son. Old pictures show Mum in a smart nurse-type uniform, complete with crisp cap, taking care of her little charge. It was a good arrangement for all concerned, and she remained with the family for two or three years.

In the meantime, one of Mum's cousins had come to the U.S. and was clerking in the baby department of Macy's in New York. As a sale was being rung up, the stylishly pregnant customer mentioned casually that she was from Atlanta, and that she would soon be needing a nanny. Jean told her she had a cousin in Toronto who was a nanny, and so after that contact, Mum took the train to Atlanta to meet the family, and was hired.

The baby was the grandson of Dr. Joseph Jacobs, a Jewish pharmacist who was instrumental in the beginnings of the Coca Cola Company. His pharmacy was the first to sell Coca Cola at their soda fountain in Atlanta where it was sampled, pronounced "excellent" and placed on sale for a few cents a glass as a soda fountain drink.

Dr. Jacobs and Daddy were close friends, belonging as they did to the Atlanta Burns Club, which Dr. Jacobs had founded. It is an association of Scottish ex-patriots and others interested in the poetry of Robert Burns. He introduced the two young people in November 1922, and when Christmas came around, Daddy, who was a frequent guest in the Jacobs' home, went around the room with gifts for all the family members. Mum was not included, as she was considered staff. But later Daddy caught her alone and had a card and gift for her.

Each Christmas as we were growing up, Daddy would scold Mum because she hadn't sent him a Christmas card that first Christmas. She would defend herself, saying she didn't think she knew him well enough to send him a card. "No," Daddy would remember, "but you knew me well enough to take a gold watch from me!" Although we had heard it numerous times and could have told the story ourselves, it would always bring hilarious giggles from us kids, as we heard our parents teasing each other. I tell people in jest that I'm a bi-product of the Coca Cola Company!

After a three-month courtship, they were married in Atlanta on March 3rd, 1923. When they came back from their honeymoon, they were guests at a reception in a beautiful Southern mansion. As the ladies gathered in the kitchen to visit with the young bride, it is amusing to me that the first topic of their conversation was "How much of Tom's leg is missing?!!" A far cry from today, when young people know all too much about each other even before they are married.

My oldest brother George was born in 1924 and Isabel came along shortly after. A couple of years later, pregnant a third time, Mum went home to Scotland and had Tommy while she was there with her parents. Returning to the States, she again became pregnant and in 1930 my sister Betty was born in Charlotte, North Carolina where Daddy was on a short-term assignment. Four children in the first six years! Maybe the family was complete?

In 1931, possibly because of the growing depression in the U.S. and after Dr. Jacobs' death, Mum and Daddy pulled up the roots they had in Atlanta and returned permanently to Scotland. They settled in Clydebank, and took over our aging Granda Ness's shop. But they never lost their love for America, and particularly the South. Most of their siblings (on both sides) had either preceded them or followed them, and their descendants are scattered all over New England as well as Georgia. Daddy's oldest brother chose farming life in Saskatchewan, Canada.

In our family, America was frequently in the conversation, and my folks retained many of their Southern habits. Although they never lost their Scottish accents (even after 23 years for Daddy), there were many Americanisms that were part and parcel of our living. Supper was not a word used in Britain, but we had supper. And my oldest sister was often addressed as "Sister" or "Sis", which I believe hearkened back to the South in those days. We children were often addressed as "Sugar," and we were often entertained with tales of their lives in "the States." In 1936 another girl, Jessie, was added to the family, and I followed 17 months later, the last in the brood of Scotts.

Daddy's leg continued to give him trouble, and over the years he had several operations in which more of the leg was removed, until eventually it was taken off a few inches below his hip. After one of Daddy's many trips to hospital in Glasgow, Betty remembers as a young girl, maybe ten years old, answering the front doorbell. It was the delivery man from the railway. He handed her a long cardboard box, quite heavy and almost as tall as she was, and with hardly an explanation, said "Here's your daddy's leg, hen." "Okay," she answered, and with that he turned and left her holding the new leg!

During the depression in the 1930s, which had also affected Scotland, it was a job to keep six children fed and clothed. Few people had cars in those days, and when Mum needed to go to Daddy's shop, she would take the bus; but things got so tight, she often walked the mile and a half to save bus fare.

Daddy gave Mum money to take care of groceries and household needs, and all her life she kept a diary of the important things she did each day. At that time, she also kept a very detailed record of whatever money she spent, down to the penny. One day when Mum was tallying her expenses, Daddy looked over her shoulder and complimented her on her excellent bookkeeping skills.

"You do a splendid job of taking care of things, Mum."

She thanked him, and then he asked her,

"But I notice every now and again you have an item LOK. What is that?"

"Oh that's part of my excellent bookkeeping skills," she responded with a smile. "It stands for Lord Only Knows!"

Meditations

Our home was not like the Leave it to Beaver home; we had the usual sibling fusses, but because of the difference in ages they were usually between Jessie and me, and sometimes Betty. Jessie was very neat. 'Nuff said! My parents were respected, and there was never any fear that we would not always be a family. Sadly, many of the problems that we see rising today stem from the fact that lots of young people don't have that reassurance.

Exodus 20:12
Honor your father and your mother, that your days may be long upon the land which the LORD your God is giving you.

Psalm 112:1
Praise the LORD! Blessed is the man who fears the LORD, who delights greatly in His commandments.

Proverbs 31:10, 27-28
Who can find a virtuous wife? For her worth is far above rubies…She watches over the ways of her household…her children rise up and call her blessed; Her husband also, and he praises her.

CHAPTER 6

Where was God in all of this?

MY PARENTS WERE certainly what I would call God-fearing. They honored the Lord's Day, and were in church most every Sunday. We were involved in the Church of Scotland, which is Presbyterian in organization. Our church was not what would be called evangelical, but it was a big influence in my growing-up years.

My earliest awareness of God was when I was about five or six. I remember standing in the kitchen in front of Mum, and she was cupping my chin in her hand. "Do you know that God lets mothers know when their child is telling lies? He makes your face turn red." It made a big impression on my young mind! I figured that even if I could trick someone else, I could never get one over on God.

We were taught as little kids to pray the Now I Lay Me Down to Sleep prayer, and I remember after that I would recite all the family members' names, including Granny Ness and Granda and Granny Scott and Granda. God must have smiled, as Granda Scott had already been gone for 50 years or more!

This continued until about the time I started high school, because I remember as Isabel married and had children, I had to fit them in to my list! I'm glad God doesn't get confused, because Isabel's husband and son were both called George. So it was God Bless George (my deceased brother), Isabel, George, and wee George! Jessie and I shared a bed in those years. We would each say our prayers silently, and when we were finished, we'd knock on the headboard of the bed to let the other one know when we were finished. Then we could play word games or talk before we went to sleep.

As a teenager, I remember hearing a man on the bus using Jesus' name as a curse word. I was absolutely stunned. Swearing was unknown in our home. The one and only time I heard Daddy swear was when he and I were by the cook stove in the scullery and he raised his head hard against an open cupboard door. "Damn!" It was out before he could stop it, and immediately he apologized to me.

Mum must have had some Christian influence in her younger years, because she would never touch a drop of wine, even at New Year's, which for Scottish people was a bigger celebration than Christmas. It had something to do with what she called the Rechabites, which was some kind of a temperance society. She was often heard singing hymns that we didn't sing at church, although she sang those too. I never hear Blessed Assurance without thinking about Mum. It was one of her favorites.

As I got into my teen years, God was becoming more and more real to me, even though I didn't yet have a relationship with Him. I remember a retreat for girls where I felt God's presence, but didn't know what it was. I just knew there was a sweetness about the service that made me want to shed tears.

I tried to read my Bible some, although Bibles in our home were generally just for church use. I remember a speaker at our youth group who was visiting from an evangelical church. He told about the young people in his area, who were going after God in a serious way. They even read their Bibles every day! He stopped there, and pointing right at me, he asked, "Do you read your Bible every day?" I answered yes, although I was thoroughly embarrassed to say that in front of everyone, especially the boys. Because I had said I did, after that evening I tried not to miss reading the Scriptures daily.

Church was very much a part of our home life. Not necessarily God, but Church. Our friends were all in our youth group, and my folks made sure our home was the one where kids usually congregated. We had great times! We often had get-togethers after our Youth Group meetings on Sunday evening. Glenfender was often packed with 10 or 12 young people, and it was something we all looked forward to and enjoyed. This was where dating started, and it usually consisted of holding hands in the company of a dozen others and a brief kiss on the lips when they weren't looking!

So high school came and went, and at sixteen I put in a work application at the National Coal Board in Glasgow, a huge government agency. I assume they decided they could fit me in somewhere, and I was hired as a shorthand typist, although at that time I didn't know shorthand, and had never touched a typewriter. I sat down the first day and tried to type the way I played the piano—with all ten fingers at once. Initially, I did a lot of copying and tea-making! Of course, that didn't continue for long, and for the three years I worked there, I attended night school three nights a week. So I did eventually become proficient at both shorthand and typing.

About the time I started at the Coal Board, our choir at church would finish each service with a beautiful quiet melody taken from Psalm 139.

Search me, O God, and know my heart;
Try me, and know my thoughts;
And see if there be any wicked way in me,
And lead me in the way, in the way everlasting.

I loved that song, and God used it to speak to me. It truly was my prayer, as He was drawing me closer to Himself. On one of his trips to Scotland, my Uncle Jimmy in Atlanta had given me a beautiful watch, but because of the pounding you had to do on the ancient typewriters they had, I was afraid it would damage the watch. So I took it off daily when I got to work and kept it in its case on my desk. I typed the words of that chorus on a small piece of paper and laid it in the watch box so I could see the words throughout the day.

About this time, we first heard about Billy Graham, and it was huge news when he held a crusade for several weeks in 1955 in Glasgow's Kelvin Hall. My girlfriend, Helen, and I took the bus to town, and joined the thousands of people filling the huge auditorium. I remember the large banner over the platform, Jesus is the Way, the Truth and the Life. As the invitation was given, Helen went forward, but I didn't feel persuaded to follow her.

Jessie's friend, Emma, and I took the train to Glasgow each day. The fun part of riding the train was the camaraderie we enjoyed with our fellow passengers. Since most people stood about the same place on the platform and the train stopped at approximately the same place, we had acquired "train buddies," a strange conglomeration of two older men, two young mid-twenties engineer types, teenagers (as we were) and a couple of thirty-something business women heading to and from work. We all knew each other by name, where they worked, who their families consisted of, and what their plans were for the weekend. It was rare that we couldn't connect with our group.

Fergus Wilson, one of the young engineers who was part of our group, attended a Mission Hall, and was a devout Christian. He got tickets for the folks in our train group to attend a Billy Graham film that Yoker Mission was showing. Emma and I were the only ones of the bunch that took him up on the offer and went to the film.

The small church was almost full, and we could tell that most of the folks were people who regularly attended there. When they gave the invitation, the pastor had the congregation sing the song "just one more time," several times over. It never dawned on us that they could be waiting for us to respond. After all, we were regular church attenders and were waiting for some real sinners to come forward!

Meditations

There were several opportunities at that time for the enemy of our souls to try to direct my life away from God. I had a lovely friend at work who invited me out for a drink one evening after work. I accepted, but was not inclined to "have another drink" when she did. And don't ask me how or why, but I found myself one day going with some other friends to visit a palm reader! On another occasion, some of us decided we'd visit other "churches" just to see what they did, and we had our eyes opened to what they called "church." One time we found we were at a séance! Each time, I know God had angels protecting not just me but my friends from evil influences.

I'm very thankful to God for even the basic teaching that we had at home, so I could make a way to walk away when I had gotten into some very wrong places.

Isaiah 44:3
For I will pour water on him who is thirsty, and floods on the dry ground; I will pour My Spirit on your descendants, and My blessing on your offspring.

Psalm 19:7, 8, 10
The law of the LORD is perfect, converting the soul;...The statutes of the LORD are right, rejoicing the heart;...More to be desired are they than gold, yea, than much fine gold; sweeter also than honey and the honeycomb.

Two Views of the Debris Next Door

George with Jessie & Dorothy

Dad & Mum

George at 19

Tommy at 19

Mum – "Only a Faded Rose!"

Precious Bible Club Children

Glenfender on the Right Today

South View Today

Bob and Dorothy

Dad and Mum on their 50th Anniversary

Dear Isabel

We Three!   Dorothy, Jessie and Betty

CHAPTER 7

The nest is getting empty

SHORTLY AFTER STARTING work at the National Coal Board, my boss called me into his office, and told me about a program they offered to give city girls a chance to get out into the countryside. As a result of that, I spent an amazing vacation at Glenmore Lodge near Aviemore, in the Cairngorm Mountain region in northern Scotland.

We spent our days learning how to sail, and were able to get fairly proficient at rigging sails on the small boats they had on Loch Morlich. We also hiked all over the mountain range that surrounded the area, and climbed the highest mountain, Cairngorm, which is over 4,000 feet. (To keep things in perspective, the highest mountain in Britain, Ben Nevis, is 4,409 feet.) Of course everything we did was accompanied by experienced leaders. It was a life-expanding experience for me, and I spent the next three years enjoying other outdoor recreational activities with the Glasgow Glenmore Club.

One trip that stands out in my memory is a time when the Club was having a weekend get-together in Callander. Daddy drove me to the Glasgow train station to catch the 6:00 AM train. There were about seven of us, and the plan was to take the train to a station ten miles from Callander and trek over the mountains to meet the others at a lodge.

Well, by noon the skies started getting very dark and the weather got worse by the minute, and then the rain started. Soon the fog and clouds were so low we could barely see the person in front of us. Although it wasn't rock climbing, it became very treacherous with lots of crevasses. Thankfully two of the men had a great deal of experience and knew how to read their compasses. I know if that hadn't been the case, we may not have survived the rugged terrain, but they weren't a bit worried and got us there by early evening. A *very* long day! I never did tell my folks about it, because they would have worried every time we went out. A friend and I hitch-hiked home from Callander.

After a couple of years, Mr. Kinnaird again called me into his office. This time it was to ask me if I would be interested in going to the University of Glasgow. The Coal Board would pay for my education and all expenses if I would commit to working for them for three years following graduation. I didn't even tell him I'd let him know, but kindly declined the offer there and then. More schooling was the last thing I wanted at that time, probably because there was something more exciting that was starting to form in the back of my mind. My dad was NOT happy with me that evening!

When I was 18, Jessie and I were the only two still at home, the others having all found mates and married. My brother Tommy had gone to Canada, and was planning to have his wife Ina and two pre-school girls, Jean and Margaret, join him once he got settled. One evening Mum and Daddy said they wanted to talk with me, and it sounded very serious.

Well, the big news was that Jessie was going to go with Ina and the girls, to help her with the children on the ship, and help get them settled. It was the summer of 1956. I was excited for her, but it made me think it sounded like a pretty good idea! I asked if I could go along, but was told that all the plans had been made and the fares paid, but if I still wanted to go later, they would certainly consider it.

Part of what made it okay for me to wait was because that summer I had my first real boyfriend! Alec was tall, not dark, but handsome, and a very sweet guy. We dated for a few months, but other things came up, and eventually we broke up. He later married one of the church girls, and sadly died very suddenly in his early twenties with a brain tumor.

So with Jessie and Tommy and his family in Canada, and with letters going in both directions, I renewed my interest in emigrating, and made plans to go the following summer. Emma was also wanting to go, so together we gradually collected passports, fares, etc. My folks were quite excited for me because of their own experiences, and their expanded view of what life could be like outside of Clydebank.

Part of the preparation involved getting appropriate luggage, and I needed a cabin trunk. Several months before our sailing date, my mother and I had gone on the hunt for a suitable cabin trunk. New ones were out of the question, so we browsed ads and used goods stores without much luck. Then one day we decided to check out one advertised in Glasgow.

It was in a questionable area, but we climbed the two floors up in a dilapidated close and knocked on the door. We noticed the peeling paint and small graffiti as we waited. The man who answered seemed decent enough, and we went in to check out the cabin trunk.

There was an untidy conglomeration of other things—dust-covered furniture, luggage, lamps and such. But the trunk was just what we had been looking for, so we paid for it and got out as quickly as possible. We each held a leather strap on the ends of this massive thing, about the size of a small coffin. The car was parked two blocks away, and even with nothing in it, it was quite heavy.

The trunk was in good shape, although it had obviously been well traveled, and had remnants of old labels that I scraped off. It had to hold all my worldly goods, except for what I wanted to have with me on board the ship. In spite of its name, it wasn't allowed in the cabin. So over the last few weeks before leaving I had gradually made decisions about what would be going and what would be left. By the time it left for shipping, I don't think there was a thimble's worth of room left in the trunk. It had its own set of stick-on labels.

My suitcase was another matter. I had carefully chosen the things I thought I'd need for the week we'd be on board. As I was about to close the lid, my mother, who had been shadowing me for days knowing we'd soon be thousands of miles apart, and cherishing every moment we had, noticed a dress I had made when I was 15. I had chosen stiff white fabric, probably taffeta, with enormous purple flowers all over it. I may have worn it once, but it was UGLY.

"You should take it – you never know, you might need it some day."

"Mum, I'm NOT taking that dress. It's dreadful, ugly, I haven't worn it and won't wear it over there."

"You'd better take it. Some day you might be glad to have another dress."

Well, after some time of back and forth, she won the argument and the dress was the last thing to go in. More about the dress later.

Meditations

Why climb the mountains?
I like to leave my littleness behind
In the low vale, where little cares are great
And in the mighty map of things to find
The lowly measure of my scanty state
Taught by the vastness of God's pictured plan
In this big world, how small a thing is man.

I found this verse underneath a picturesque mountain scene in a climbing book, and have been unsuccessful in finding its source. I didn't intentionally memorize it, but turned to it so often it has affixed itself in my mind for more than 60 years. It reminds me of a favorite verse:

Psalm 121:1
I will lift up my eyes to the hills—From whence comes my help? My help comes from the LORD, Who made heaven and earth.

CHAPTER 8

Day of Departure - July 26, 1957

AFTER MONTHS OF preparation, the day finally dawned that would mark a dividing line in my life. It was a dismal morning, not raining yet but with the low-hanging clouds and the dampness in the air, we knew it would be soon. My folks had called a taxicab, even though it was just a short distance to the train station. Daddy's leg made walking very far a bit of a trial, and with cases and purses, umbrellas and people, a taxi was a better choice.

We pulled up outside Emma's home at 10 South View and waited in the taxi. South View was a short road just around the corner from our home. It didn't have Street or Road after it, just South View that had been part of my growing-up neighborhood. I had walked by the homes hundreds of times on the way to Primary School. I always enjoyed that walk.

There were seven identically-styled semi-detached buildings, two stories graystone, with high peaked architecture. Each had a low stone wall along the front, with the tell-tale stubs of steel still showing in the stone, a remnant of the war effort that had never been corrected. The yards were tidy and all the lawns were carefully mowed and manicured. The homes were all on the north side of the road, and across from them was a tall iron paling. Beyond it, the mowed grass-covered ground descended to where the train tracks lay, out of sight of the homes.

I noticed that even though it was broad daylight, one rebellious street light was still shining. As kids, we had often trailed behind the lamplighter as he pushed his rod up into the cute Dickens-style gas lamps each evening. But a few years prior to this, they had been replaced in our neighborhood by these ugly tall street lights.

Emma's parents didn't want to go with us, just wanted to say their goodbyes at home. After a few minutes wait, she came out with her suitcase in one hand, her other arm holding her purse, an umbrella and her raincoat slung over it. Her folks waved us goodbye from their doorway. Emma's face was tear-streaked as she climbed into the back of the taxi and pulled down the jump seat behind the driver. There wasn't much conversation, just a quick hello how are you, and the taxi drove the short distance to the station.

The train wasn't in, so we found seats on the slatted wooden benches in the waiting room. Daddy was never one to leave things to the last minute and we had left ample time for getting there, Even though it was late July, there was a distinct chill in the air, and the station seemed even colder than outside. I didn't know if the shiver I felt was because of nerves or the temperature.

The station was probably about seventy-five years old, with all the accoutrements of an ancient rail road. The huge clock hanging on the wall told us we had almost fifteen minutes to wait, leaving plenty of time to stop at the polished wooden desk for tickets. Of the four, only two of them would be return tickets. We were all pretty quiet, but the time passed quickly and we soon heard the approaching train, and could feel the vibrations in the station floor as it came nearer.

Emma and I were very used to this routine, as both of us had traveled to work daily from this very station platform. We bought monthly passes and the trip took us about 45 minutes to get to Queen Street Station. If the weather permitted, we would roll down the window, using the wide leather strap that hooked on to a metal peg below the window. But once we got closer to Glasgow, the window would have to be closed, as the last part of the trip was underground, and the tunnels would fill with dirty black smoke from the train.

But there wasn't time for reminiscing that morning. We were headed not to Glasgow, but in the opposite direction. The train's destination was Helensburgh, and after boarding in Dalmuir, we immediately began passing through beautiful country and the villages that sprinkled the area. Rich green fields spread out towards the west, until they merged with the hills that lined the horizon on the other side of the river. We made stops in Old Kilpatrick, Bowling, Dumbarton, Dalreoch, Cardross, and Craigendoran, where we got off, just short of the final stop. It took us about an hour.

As we went along we didn't notice many other people boarding the train, but when we got off there were a number of people who had labels on their luggage similar to ours. Large labels declared we were CUNARD LINE passengers, and this case would be NEEDED ON BOARD and my last initial was a gigantic S for Scott. Absent from this batch of luggage were our cabin trunks, which had been sent ahead. They would already have been loaded by a derrick into a huge hold on the main deck of the ship, and would not be seen by us until we docked in Canada.

So here we were in Craigendoran. The ship was leaving from Greenock, which was on the other side of the River Clyde, immediately across from Craigendoran. Most people from Glasgow would go down to Greenock, but there was a small vessel that would take passengers over there from the east bank of the river.

We had been told we had to be on the pier ready to leave at noon, but it was only ten o'clock. So we went into a small tea room, sparkling clean but no quaint theme like lighthouses or windmills. We whiled away an hour or so, passing the time with last-minute things. When the waitress checked our tea supply for the third time, we decided we had better leave and head down to the pier. There was a shelter there where we could wait, and Cunard people were there to help with any questions we had.

Finally it was time to leave, and of course the leaving then was so hard. I had lived at home all of my 19 years, and was the last of six to leave the nest. I was finally leaving home, and my poor parents were crying as they said goodbye to their youngest. It was a sad time, and by then the skies had gotten grayer than ever and it was raining steadily. We hugged, walked away a few steps, then hurried back for more hugs, and finally we left, turning around every few steps to get in one last wave. I knew then why Emma had been crying.

Meditations

At that time, my walk with God was not close. So I can't say I was very aware of the way He was leading my life. I was just an excited teenager, headed out on a huge adventure, following thousands of other Scottish young people who were emigrating to see what else the world had to offer. Although I didn't give it much thought, I knew I could always come back home if this didn't work out. But I was going to give it a good try.

During the last year after Jessie left, I remember some very cozy talks with Mum about a number of things, including Alec. She assured me that there would be other young men coming in and out of my life. No doubt as we were talking from time to time, she was reminiscing about her own experiences 37 years earlier. She had shared the same wanderlust that I had, but I had no idea that Toronto would not be the last stop in the road for me.

Deuteronomy 31:6
Be strong and of good courage, do not fear nor be afraid of them; for the LORD your God, He is the One who goes with you. He will not leave you nor forsake you.

CHAPTER 9

Vessel of Change

On deck I stand
            Alone
The skies above let fall upon the depths of seas
A contribution to their unmeasured fullness
And from my eyes to match the rain
    a tear, and still another fall upon my coat
And through a mist
Whether of tears or of the atmosphere I cannot tell
I see the shore, so far and yet so near
    a link with childhood yet
And out ahead a giant lives, unknown to me
The future, veiled in dark obscurity

You knew back then, O Lord, it held my liberty
Not cast in stone, but in a heart set free
So now I look, back from that distant shore
Give thanks to God, and shed a tear once more

EMMA AND I picked our steps carefully over rain-slicked planks that looked like they could have been part of the Ark. At the end of the pier, we were ushered on to a shaky gangplank and boarded a small charter boat that had been ferrying passengers over to the ship for the last hour or two. We could see the *RMS Carinthia* in the distance, and even in the rain she looked like a sparkling jewel sitting on an old piece of gray velvet. As we approached Greenock, she looked large though not extremely so. But the closer we got the more immense the ship got, and when we pulled up alongside, we felt like we were standing next to a 15-story building. The front and back of the ship disappeared into the rain.

After landing at the pier, we joined hundreds of other excited passengers and families who were hugging and saying their goodbyes. There were lots of families with young children, as well as young singles and middle aged folks. We walked up the gangplank, and now we were on board, with guidance from some Cunard people. Our cases were brought up behind us and were taken immediately to our assigned cabin.

My first impression was that the ship was enormous. I could hardly believe that something like this could float, let alone sail thousands of miles. For some reason I was fascinated by the rivets—not like any rivets I'd seen before. They were at least an inch and a half across, and there were thousands of them everywhere. Although the sides of the ship were painted shiny black, most everything else was white, and it looked like the thick paint itself could have held the ship together. A strip about fifteen feet above the water line was painted red that matched the red on the funnel.

The *RMS Carinthia* had just lately been built for Cunard Line, not more than two miles from where we had started that morning. It wasn't her maiden voyage, but she was less than a year old, a beautiful liner. If she had been a racehorse, she would have come from the same purebred stables as the Queen Mary, Queen Elizabeth, and the Royal Yacht Britannia, in John Brown's Shipyards in Clydebank. Boys we had flirted with in high school had helped build her, and my mother's uncle was the chief fireman for John Brown's.

Unlike the Queens, she had one single funnel, red at the lower end and black above. It soared above the mid-ship area. Like the Queens, she had been christened and launched by a member of the Royal Family, Princess Margaret. I remembered in primary school, we used to get out of class when ships were launched so we could line the streets and wave small Union Jacks at whatever Royal was in town. When the Carinthia was launched there was a crowd of 20,000 flag-waving locals, workers, and excited school kids jammed into every nook and cranny inside Brown's, cheering at the ceremony. A launch was always the biggest event in town.

The Carinthia was the third of four sister ships built in Clydebank in the early 1950s to accommodate the huge numbers of Scots who were emigrating. War-weary Britain was paying the price yet again, losing many young people and families who wanted to find new life and excitement in Canada.

Now that we were on board, we were guided into a line that had formed outside the purser's office. It snaked along one wall and around a corner, but it moved quite quickly. They mostly checked our identity, comparing our information with what they had listed on long sheets of names, looked at our passports, changed pounds into dollars, asked if we had any valuables we wanted stored (we had none), and issued our cabin keys.

Daddy had given me 50 pounds, about ten times my weekly salary. It was the most money I'd ever had, but I wasn't about to hand it over to some stranger. I'd wait until I could change it at a bank. It would have to last me until I got settled and found a job. As the minutes passed, the sadness and longing for my parents gradually receded and were replaced by excitement and anticipation, as the reality of what we were doing grew inside me.

We finally started looking for our cabin. Yes, there was the little brass plate C113, with our cases sitting outside. We found the door already unlocked, and as we entered we were stunned at how small the cabin was. There were two sets of bunks, as we had been assigned a room with two older ladies. One of the ladies was there, and we introduced ourselves to Mildred. With graying hair and a fresh perm, not a hair out of place, we guessed her somewhere in her mid-fifties.

We divvied up the minimal drawer space that was available, and stacked our suitcases where we could use them as needed. During the day they laid on our bunks. A tiny bathroom was tucked in a nook. In the main cabin, we pulled down the large brass lever and looked out the porthole at the vast water we were floating on. That was the first time I noticed the movement of the River Clyde beneath us.

The ship was not due to sail until mid-afternoon, so we spent more time looking around the ship. The corridors were pretty crowded as we passed lots of other passengers who were exploring, as we were. We occasionally had to grasp the railing as the ship's gentle motion shifted us from side to side. We came on a large open area, kind of an atrium at least three decks high, with a palatial wide-curved staircase with sparkling white banisters. We were told the first-class dining room was upstairs.

We snooped in the halls, then headed back to our cabin, kicked off our shoes, and tried the bunks. They were adequate, but certainly not plush. However, we were just glad to be on our way, after months of planning. We were too excited to nap (teenagers don't nap!), but we spent a while just talking about the morning and what lay ahead.

After a while, we started hearing the crew shouting orders, so we decided to go up on deck and watch the activity as they pulled up the anchor, and almost unnoticeably we were under way. As I stood looking across the water, it seemed as if the sky and sea met in their grayness. If there was a line where they divided, it was blurred by the rain, falling steadily on waters that were churning with the ship's engines. I wept a little, but the tears went unnoticed on my face and coat, both now wet with the rain.

As the ship turned, we caught a hazy glimpse of the shore where we had stood so recently, and now it seemed as distant as eternity. I knew for sure my parents were there, crowded with the other families on the pier, no doubt waving in our direction. They were symbols of what had gone before. We waved back, but excitement about the future waiting beyond the days of traveling on the ocean, took over our emotions.

Again, the poem at the start of this chapter was written in about 15 minutes, as an assignment in a Creative Writing class in college, about 1965.

Meditations

Emigration from Scotland was huge in the 1950s, and several of my schoolmates also left home, some to South Africa, Australia, or New Zealand, but mostly to Canada. Actually, it was not only in the 1950s, but for decades thousands from all over Europe had been leaving to populate the New World. Only one of Emma's three siblings remained in Scotland.

At one point in our family, the three of us born in Scotland were living in Canada, while the two (not counting George) born in the U.S. were living in Scotland. Truly a mixed up international bunch! I remember our family crowding around our phone on an international call. It cost a lot for three minutes, and the extent of each one's conversation was mostly "Hello" and "'Bye – here's Mum" depending on who was next in line. Not a lot of information was transmitted by phone.

Psalm 104:24-26
O LORD, how manifold are Your works! In wisdom You have made them all. The earth is full of Your possessions—This great and wide sea, in which are innumerable teeming things, Living things both small and great. There the ships sail about.

CHAPTER 10

On the High Seas in the 1950s

Back in the cabin, we primped a bit and headed to the dining room. We had chosen the early seating, so we walked around and found the table that had been assigned to us. The table service sparkled—shiny silver-plate alongside bone china dishes, all with the Cunard insignia. As we sat there, still at last, we could feel the motion of the ship, even though the stabilizers kept it at a minimum. At first we thought the waiters were a bit stiff and formal, but we soon learned that underneath their formal black and white attire were everyday people. Most of them had English accents, which made them seem more proper.

The meal had several courses, each one delicious. The menu was mostly in foreign languages, and I recognized some words from my high school French. I figured the other language was Italian. We tried to guess what it was and knew we would not be disappointed. This was going to be fun! After dinner, we were informed about events in the various public areas about what we could expect on board, lifeboat drills, and details about tours of the ship etc. We finally called it a day and headed back to the cabin.

I woke up early the next morning, and was shocked to hear Emma moaning and groaning in the lower bunk. Yes, she was seasick, with a capital S! And it continued until the day before we docked. Poor girl, she missed almost all the delicious meals, and I didn't miss a one. I felt sorry for her, but ended up going on my own until I made friends with a couple of other young people. Of course, I'd check back at the cabin numerous times throughout the day, but the activities available were too much fun to miss.

Generally in the evening Emma would manage to get up for a bit, and we'd go out on deck to get fresh air and watch the ocean. The air did her good, and she enjoyed being out of the cabin. The ocean was truly awe-inspiring, stretching to the horizon in every direction. We were fairly far north, about the same latitude as southern Alaska, so daylight lasted until about ten o'clock.

On one of those nights, closer to 10:30 or 11 pm, we heard some kind of faint music above the swishing of the ocean and the constant muffled hum of the ship's engine. We followed it to the stern of the main deck and were delightfully surprised to find a band of sorts, made up of cabin and kitchen help, with a hilarious assortment of instruments and vocalists. I distinctly remember the double bass fiddle, anchored on the bottom with a large wooden box with a two-by-four nailed to it, strung with guitar strings and played with real skill! The other instruments were equally innovative, and they actually made some real music, which entertained a growing number of passengers as the word was spread around during the week. I was glad Emma felt good enough in the evenings to enjoy that part.

It was after one of these impromptu midnight concerts that we observed another amazing fact about trans-ocean liners in the 1950s. Shortly after midnight, several crew members came to the very back of the main deck, hauling enormous black bags filled with the day's trash produced by a thousand people. And yes, over the rail they went to make their way to the bottom of the North Atlantic! Most of the passengers slept through this ritual, totally unaware of the drama taking place above them. So the breeze that carried the music harmlessly from the stern of the ship also carried unknown amounts of trash to a watery grave!

The rest of the week passed uneventfully, and there was great excitement when the buzz went around the ship that land could be seen. By this time Emma was more like herself and could enjoy the adventure. We hurried to the deck and sure enough with a little imagination we could see what appeared to be land, still probably at least 75 miles or more in the distance. At last, Canada! It was so exciting to watch the land gradually take shape to where you could make out definite hills and shoreline.

As it turned out, the land we were watching appear before our eyes was Newfoundland and Labrador, and we passed this province that sounds like two, and entered the St. Lawrence River.

Although it felt like we should be getting off very soon, we enjoyed watching as the ship maneuvered the St. Lawrence. The River quickly narrowed so we could watch towns and villages meander past us. So far we liked what we saw of Canada!

It took a full day to reach Quebec City, where we docked for a good part of the day. Some passengers disembarked, but mostly it was time spent off-loading and restocking supplies. We did get off, our first steps on a new continent, and took a bus to the Chateau Frontenac, which dominated the city just north of downtown. We had fun practicing our French, and it was a beautiful palace, but we were too excited to be in Canada to be too impressed with its architecture, and we soon returned to the ship.

That evening after the farewell dinner, we returned to our cabin to start packing for real. We would be docking early the next morning. Over the course of the week, we had picked up some things in the shops on board, not really thinking about how we were going to pack them. So when it came time to close my case for our final destination, it was clear that something had to go. You've guessed it. The dress! Sorry, Mum, there just wasn't room for the dress, and I kept it out trying to decide how to dispose of it. So under cover of darkness on our last evening on board, I opened the porthole and the dress floated down into the St. Lawrence. I just hoped nobody would find it and start looking for a body!

When we woke the next morning, we could tell something was different. The engines were still humming, and we were still rocking slightly, but we weren't moving! We had docked in Montreal, the ship's final destination. We went to the dining room for breakfast, and listened to all the directions that were being broadcast. We said our goodbyes to the two lovely ladies who had shared our cabin, and had been so kind to Emma in her distress, and followed the crowd to the gangplank where we would leave our beautiful ship for the last time. Canada, here we come!

Epilogue for this chapter:

Fast forward to 1994; my husband Bob and I took our first cruise, down the Mexican Riviera from Los Angeles. As we approached the dock where the Fair Princess was tied up, we were entertained by wonderful Mexican musicians. We were really looking forward to a fun week. My husband asked me in passing how the ship compared to the one that brought me to Canada, and my answer was that the Carinthia was much larger than this. We boarded and found our cabin.

About the third day into our cruise, as we were enjoying the beautiful Mexican sunshine, we decided to take a tour of the bridge. When the crowd had gathered, they passed out a sheet of paper that gave the history of the ship and I was absolutely astounded to read the first words. *"The Fair Princess was built at John Brown's Shipyards in Clydebank, Scotland for Cunard Line. At that time she was launched by Princess Margaret and named The Carinthia."* TRUE STORY! I was once again back on board my beloved *Carinthia*. I felt like going out and hugging the funnel! After several years with Cunard, she had been sold to the Sitmar Cruise Line, and sailed the Mediterranean for some time before being purchased along with her sister ships by Princess. We were told that this was to be her last cruise for Princess in Mexico. We heard she sailed one more season in Alaska before being sold to a company in the Far East, but her history after that is a blur.

The rest of the cruise was just plain fun, as I tried to remember which cabin we were in, and how we now had access to the beautiful dining room that had been reserved for first class passengers.

There was something about it, though, that I couldn't figure out. There were two swimming pools on the Fair Princess, and I knew there were none on the Carinthia. One night I was lying in my bunk and it dawned on me why the swimming pools were strange, being the same depth everywhere, with no shallow or deep end. They had converted the large hold where our cabin trunks had been into the main swimming pool! And on one of the upper decks there was a small paddling pool for children.

It also was of one depth, and no doubt had been converted from some other use.

Although some of the passengers complained that the Fair Princess was not as up to date as some other ships, the cruise became for me a treasure trove of memories. There were now probably numerous coats of heavy white paint, and the portholes were no longer operable, but we could still go to the stern of the ship and in my mind's ear I could hear once again the music of strange instruments that had lingered for thirty seven years.

Meditations

It certainly is amazing to stand on the deck of an ocean liner, look in every direction, and day after day see nothing but turbulent waters and the occasional distant iceberg. The voyage took us about seven or eight days. It wasn't frightening, but I must admit there was a sense of some relief when land was spotted.

Psalm 107:23-27
Those who go down to the sea in ships…They see the works of the LORD, and His wonders in the deep. For He commands and raises the stormy wind, which lifts up the waves of the sea. They mount up to the heavens, they go down again to the depths; their soul melts because of trouble. They reel to and fro, and stagger like a drunken man.

CHAPTER 11

Bien Venu au Canada

AFTER CORRALLING OUR luggage at the dock in Montreal, Emma and I took the train to Toronto and were met by Tommy and Jessie, and some old family friends of my parents. The first things I noticed that were really different were the cars. They were colored! Every color of the rainbow, compared with the ones in Scotland, which were all black. And of course, they were all traveling on the wrong side of the street.

When Jessie came over the previous year, she had moved in with Tommy and the family. But with our coming, she had rented a one-bedroom apartment in Mimico for the three of us girls. Amedeo Court Apartments. They sounded pretty fancy, but looking back they were just four large three-story blocks of apartments, located on the shore of Lake Ontario, just around the bay from Toronto. It was cozy living, but it worked for us for the first year.

The only occasion I had to experience flashbacks was the first time I heard a fire truck speeding along the road, with its sirens blaring. Fire trucks in Scotland had huge brass bells, and one of the firemen would create a clang, clang, clang as they raced along. I still remember the sinking turmoil I felt momentarily in my stomach as I heard what seemed like air raid sirens. It happened a few times until I got used to the Canadian fire engines.

It didn't take long for me to find a job, and I was hired as a secretary at the local branch of the YMCA for about $150 a month. We shared the building with the YWCA and had joint programs with them. Immigration was huge in Canada, and our social life centered around the YMCA Club Bien Venu, (Welcome), which consisted of all of us new immigrants, mostly from Britain and other European countries. Fun times! There were lots of other Scots, English, Italian and German young people, as well as local Canadians. One of my favorite memories was driving into Toronto every Monday evening to roller skate. There were a couple of car loads of us.

After working a few months, their Y's Men's Club decided they wanted to sponsor someone to attend a national conference that was planned for Vancouver. I don't know why, but like the Glenmore experience, they decided they would sponsor the young Scottish woman in the front office! Again, it was an amazing experience, my first flight (to Calgary) and I was able to spend a day or two at a lodge in the Rocky Mountains, before continuing the trip to Vancouver by train.

Camp Elphinstone, on Howe Sound just north of Vancouver, was where the conference was, and I thoroughly enjoyed all the activities at the conference. One funny thing that happened there was that during a program, complete with speaker, I got a very bad muscle cramp in my leg that necessitated me causing a bit of a stir. One of the guys asked me, "Whadja got, a Charlie Horse?" I didn't know what kind of horse Charlie had, I just knew I had to stretch a bit! I'd never heard the expression before.

Before returning home, I took a ferry to Victoria and spent a few days with my father's oldest sister, Aunt Phemie, and her husband Lew. I was the only one in the family who had met them, as they had emigrated many years before Daddy. Again, I felt very blessed to have this extra experience with minimal expense on my part.

Club Bien Venu frequently held dances in the YMCA which were very popular and always attracted a good crowd of young people. Because of the large number of German and Austrian immigrants, their music and dances made up a large part of the evenings. One of my most embarrassing experiences was during such a dance. In the mid-fifties, a very popular style for young ladies was a dress that could be worn with crinolines, under-slips with elastic waists, with several layers of ruffles. If you really wanted to be in style you could wear two petticoats, which would make your dress stand out beautifully.

On this particular evening, I had put on a pretty dress over two crinolines. You could say I was a stand-out! Well, the MC announced a polka and of course all the Germans were on the floor and a young man and I joined them for the dance. This was the original Fast and Furious!

We went whirling around the hall, thoroughly enjoying the skipping and fun that polkas demand. All of a sudden, I felt something bothering me, and I looked down to find that the two crinolines had decided they'd had enough polka, and were making their way to the floor! I quickly excused myself and headed for the nearest escape, which was the door into the kitchen. I hauled the crinolines back up and made it through the rest of the evening, courtesy of two borrowed safety pins. But no more polkas that night!

Jessie and Emma were both working in downtown Toronto, but I was fortunate to be traveling just a ten minute ride to work in the other direction. As winter approached that first year, I noticed something strange as I traveled on the street-car into New Toronto to work. It was only about a mile or two, but at one of the main intersections, something was changing on an empty corner. I went home and told the girls, "They're planting some kind of a forest at that intersection. All kinds of trees are there now." It was my introduction to Christmas tree lots. And of course after Christmas, the trees were gone and the empty lot returned to its former boring condition.

That Christmas in 1957, the office staff at the YMCA were having a Christmas party at the downtown headquarters, and I remember that event because it was the first time I heard the song O Holy Night. Glenna Davis had the voice of an angel as she sang for us. I was finding out that many hymns and carols that had been standard fare at home were totally unknown on this side of the Atlantic.

After about a year, Jessie became engaged, and as plans were made for her wedding, I moved into New Toronto. I rented a room in a home with an elderly lady, Mrs. Mimms, who lived on Fifth Street, what the locals called Firemen's Row, as most of the homes were owned by firemen. I was one of three boarders, so for $80 a month I had my own room and delicious meals. The other two boarders were a middle aged lady, who was dance crazy, and a male high school teacher, who sometimes corrected my English. I was still learning the nuances and idioms of Canadian English, and more than once it created either embarrassing or comical situations.

The first winter in Canada was not as bad as I had heard about, but the second winter it felt like the frozen north. I remember waiting for a streetcar, and crying because of the pain in my legs with the icy wind. When I woke up on Easter morning following my second winter, we had six inches of snow on the ground. I slid and pussyfooted my way four blocks to church along an unpaved path that cut through the neighborhood. Mrs. Mimms said she never took the storm windows off until the end of May. "There's always a big storm in late May," was her mantra.

Meditations

Perhaps it was partly because of being raised in a large family, but it was fairly easy for me to make friends. So the transition from Scotland to suburban Toronto was not traumatic or difficult for me.

Although his purposes and destinations were infinitely more lofty and honorable than mine, I can relate to the Apostle Paul in his travels. I'm amazed at how detailed the records are of his journeys. A good example is in Acts 20 verses 5 and 6: "These men, going ahead, waited for us at Troas. But we sailed away from Philippi after the Days of Unleavened Bread, and in five days joined them at Troas, where we stayed seven days." There are many other instances where clearly someone had made sure they checked their calendars. And it gives us great comfort to know that the Holy Scriptures were not just thrown together willy nilly. Dr. Luke kept scrupulous records of their journeys.

CHAPTER 12

On the Road Again

With Jessie now married and out of the area, the restlessness that had brought me to Canada returned, and about two years after my arrival in Canada, I applied to the United States for authority to move south of the border. It took me six months and my wonderful cousins in the Boston area became guarantors should I become destitute. They were part of the Scott side of the family who had settled in New England. My mother's relatives are mostly in Georgia.

I crossed the border by bus at Buffalo, New York, which is stamped on my documents as my Port of Entry. I was a green card-carrying resident alien! Although I didn't know God in a personal way, He was always watching over me in all my wanderings. I moved into the Franklin Square House in Boston, an enormous residence for about 600 single women. It was later featured as a hospital in the 1980s television series St. Elsewhere. We all had our private rooms, and gathered in a huge dining area for meals.

My cousins lived in Needham, a beautiful little town a few miles from the city, while the Franklin Square House was in a pretty seedy area of South Boston. So every chance I got, I spent the weekends in Needham. It was what you picture when you think of New England—brick country church with a white steeple and beautiful tree-lined streets.

As was my habit, even though I was new to Boston I started looking for a church fairly close to where we lived. (By that time I had forgotten all about reading the Bible every day.) I settled on a very famous old church not far from my home. It was rather formal, but I enjoyed the singing, especially their wonderful choir, which was located in the balcony, directly opposite the platform where the minister spoke.

After a couple of months, I made inquiries about singing in the choir, and after a brief audition was told when the rehearsals were. It was not a huge choir, but they were *very* good. A couple of weeks after I started, I noticed the director went around giving each one an envelope. One other gentleman and I were the only ones who didn't get an envelope. Turned out the rest of the choir were professional singers and they were getting their paychecks!

The choir loft was in the balcony, so we were pretty much out of direct vision of most of the congregation. I was surprised and somewhat amused to watch the choir, after the musical part of the worship service. When the minister got up and began his sermon, the choir members assumed different activities. Several got up and left, some got out their books and started studying, some wrote letters, and in general you could say that they were not wholly engrossed in the sermon!

At rehearsal a week or two later, the choir director passed on a comment from the pastor about the unfortunate situation in the choir, that so many seemed to be having kidney problems that required their departure from the choir loft. I don't remember that his remonstrance made much difference, although it might have been less distracting for a week or two.

After several months at Franklin Square House, four of us decided we could do better sharing an apartment. We decided on Brookline, but hadn't chosen an exact location. However, as occasion allowed and when eyes weren't looking, we would help ourselves to some of the dishes, silverware, etc. that were available for us at meals. My assignment was water glasses, and I had a stash of four of them in my room. We were furnishing our kitchen!

Our plans were put on hold over the summer, and soon changed greatly. One of the girls whom I hardly knew had a family friend who was going to drive to Portland, Oregon where she had a position teaching at Lewis and Clark College. Joyce, age 19, was to go with her, and had planned stops with relatives along the way, and somehow had a job lined up in Portland. However a few days before their departure, she received a telegram from the friend saying she didn't want the responsibility of taking her; she left as scheduled, but without Joyce.

Joyce, who had a hot temper anyway, was madder than a hornet and announced at our table that she was going anyway, if anyone wanted to join her. She had a 1953 Plymouth convertible that had been a high school graduation gift from her parents. I never did like the Boston area (although we've since had wonderful vacations there), so I told Joyce that if she would wait a couple of weeks so I could give notice at my job, I would go with her to the west coast.

On my last day of work in Boston, as one of the owners was leaving the office, he stepped to the door and tossed a last comment to me. "Goodbye, Scotty. I hope you find what you're looking for in Portland—a man." I was a bit insulted with his remark. He had no idea what my social life was like, either in Toronto or Boston. I certainly had my share of dates, but marriage was the last thing I was looking for. However, I found out later that he was right. I *was* looking for a Man, and I was to find Him in Portland.

Meditations

The year I spent in Boston was a period I recall with few fond memories. Apart from the good times I had with the Needham cousins, and cousins in Rhode Island, I think I felt I was losing the anchor of family. I began to participate in activities that I would never have considered prior to that time. The water glasses were an example of this. However, God would never let me get too far afield of His plan, and Boston turned out to be a stepping stone to get me to the place He had planned all along.

Proverbs 1:8, 10, 15, 16
My son, hear the instruction of your father, and do not forsake the law of your mother…if sinners entice you, do not consent…do not walk in the way with them…for their feet run to evil.

Proverbs 19:27
Cease listening to instruction, my son, and you will stray from the words of knowledge.

CHAPTER 13

Finding What I Was Looking For

IN SEPTEMBER 1960 Joyce and I took two weeks to cross the United States. She did all the driving, as I hadn't yet learned to drive. In 90 degree weather, her snow skis were sticking out the top of the little convertible. It was a wonderful trip, as we stopped in several places to see the sights. Joyce had relatives in Wisconsin who took us to see the Wisconsin Dells, and we spent time in Yellowstone, stayed with her brother in northern Washington, and in some other states as they took our fancy.

After arriving in Portland, it took me just a few days to find a job, but Joyce was pretty unsettled. A few weeks after we arrived, she decided she didn't like Portland, and sold her car to get bus fare back to Boston. I was here by myself, and my closest relatives were on the east coast. But I loved it! My job turned out to be a blessing and I stayed with the company, sometimes part time, for about eleven years, eventually becoming a supervisor. My starting monthly salary was about $275.

I found a very lovely residence for young women, within walking distance of my job. I became friends with a girl who prayed over her meals and I was happy to accept her invitation to a Nazarene Church. In their Sunday School class, the leader mentioned John 3:16, and said "Why don't we say it together." I was shocked that everyone in the room knew that verse except me! It might as well have been a verse out of Leviticus or Jeremiah.

I later began attending First Baptist Church where I heard the Gospel preached on a regular basis. I also heard about tithes, and asked my Nazarene friend what the word meant. She explained that Christians give ten percent of their income to the Lord. "Oh really?" was my response, and from that day on, tithing was a commitment I've kept throughout my life.

I had always known about God and had a desire to become a witness but knew nothing about how to go about it. So I went to Christian Supply and bought a little book, The Art of Personal Witnessing, published by The Navigators. I was determined to answer all the questions at the end of the chapters. I got as far as the first chapter when I read that in order to be a witness, one had to have a personal relationship with Jesus.

Remembering my commitment to do the "assignments," I got down on my knees beside my bed and prayed the prayer written there, asking Jesus to forgive my sins and come into my heart and be my Savior. It was a definite act of faith on my part. There was no emotional upheaval. I got up and kept reading, not knowing my life and my eternal destiny had been changed in those few minutes! I've always felt that God used Joyce just to get me to Portland for that particular moment. I had finally found the Man I was looking for.

As an aside, in 2003 we were vacationing with my cousin Sandra, who lives in Colorado, and visited the Navigators headquarters there. I inquired in their bookstore about Lorne Sanny, the author of my little book, and asked if he was still alive. Indeed he was and he lived on the property. Both he and his wife were fighting cancer. So I purchased a post card and gave a brief testimony of how his book had affected my life 43 years before. The clerk said she would inter-office it to Mr. Sanny. I was delighted a few days later to receive a beautiful letter from him, thanking me. He told me he never felt the book had been very valuable or successful! It encouraged him so much. A couple of years later, I read in Christianity Today that he had passed on to his reward. I am very thankful I wrote that card!

Shortly after my experience with God, I came across those four plain glasses that I had toted clear across the country from Boston. Instantly the Lord convicted me of that petty thievery. I immediately sat down and wrote a check for $5 which I figured in 1960 would more than cover the cost of four plain, scratched water glasses. I enclosed it in a letter to the proprietor of the Franklin Square House, telling her of our plan and my recent experience with the Lord. By return mail, she sent a note saying in all her years she had a few times been reimbursed anonymously for similar items. But this was the first time anyone had put a name to their confession. She thanked me profusely and wished me well. I felt good about that, and donated the glasses to a local charity shop.

In the months after arriving in Portland, and seven years after leaving high school in Scotland, I began to make inquiries about continuing my education. This time I was more than ready! Because I was able to work part-time where I was employed, I chose to stay in town and spent four years at Cascade College, a small Christian liberal arts college. It was a huge blessing because it grounded me in my new-found faith. I learned so much more than psychology and calculus! I had the whole dorm and roommate experience, and watched as God provided miraculously for my tuition and fees.

The summer after my freshman year, I lived with several senior girls in Pepper Cottage, a small house on school property. But I wasn't sure I had enough funds for future tuition, and was contemplating finishing at Portland State, which would have been much cheaper. However, even as a fairly new believer I was becoming more familiar with the Bible and in my daily reading I found a scripture in Isaiah 55:1-2

> Ho! Everyone who thirsts, come to the waters; and you who have no money, come, buy and eat…without money and without price. Why do you spend money for what is not bread, and your wages for what does not satisfy? Listen carefully to Me, and eat what is good, and let your soul delight itself in abundance.

I figured I was getting "fed" well at Cascade, and the "bread" at PSU would not satisfy my hungry soul. Over the course of the summer, and after discussion with my housemates, I decided I'd stay at Cascade, and found He really does provide well for His children.

Those were wonderful years and God's Word became more and more precious. Our chapels included amazing missionary speakers including J. Edwin Orr, and Gladys Aylward (the Little Woman of the Inn of the Sixth Happiness), as well as numerous home-grown missionaries. God was quickly giving me a heart for missions, and for a year or two I felt that perhaps I was supposed to go to Africa.

Throughout the four years of college, I was involved in a group for international students. It consisted of students from several local colleges, and was the ministry of a number of couples who felt called to reach students from other countries. After all, most of the students would be returning to their own countries, and this was their way of impacting lives that would take the Gospel back to their own homes. We had week-end retreats, picnics, camping trips, and weekly Bible studies. They were great times. Every Thanksgiving they would organize a weekend get-together at a large facility on the Oregon Coast. It was so much fun!

As Christmas approached during my senior year, my Aunt and Uncle in Atlanta invited me to come spend the holidays with them. What a blessing that was! They sent me airline tickets, and let me get a taste of the area where my parents had lived in the 1920s. The trip also allowed me to stop over on the return flight to attend a missions conference in Illinois.

During the last few months in school, I was pondering what I would do after graduation. One of my friends had spent a summer at the Summer Institute of Linguistics (SIL), which was training for work in Bible translation with Wycliffe. It sounded like something I would enjoy, and wondered if this was my future. However, about that same time my parents were planning a trip to visit Jessie and her family north of Toronto. They assumed I would join the family there. I was in a real quandary.

As the weeks went by, I was still undecided. I was open to both options, but definitely wanted the one that was in God's will and prayed with diligence for God's guidance. At almost the last week or so before I had to make the choice, I was having my daily Bible reading in Deuteronomy. Again, it's not a book I would normally use to get answers, but as I was reading in Chapter 8, I was amazed to read what I realized was God's answer. The verses that stopped me cold read:

> "For the LORD your God is bringing you into a good land, a land of brooks of water...a land in which you will lack nothing...a land whose stones are iron and out of whose hills you can dig copper." Deuteronomy 8:7-9.

Jessie lived near Sudbury, about 250 miles north of Toronto. It was an area with very little vegetation because of the mining operations all through that area. I knew I had my answer, having visited the area and knowing of the copper and nickel mining that were the predominant industries. I thanked God for His guidance, and booked a flight. Although I was still a relatively young Christian, I was beginning to make the Bible my roadmap in life.

I knew it was not possible for my parents to come to Portland for my graduation. However, my Aunt May flew up from Atlanta for that weekend. So even after several decades, their family was continuing to bless our family.

Instead of SIL, I spent part of the summer enjoying the family and returned and started working part time with the Union Gospel Mission in their Child Evangelism area. Each weekday we had after-school Bible clubs all over the inner city areas. Much of the time the children opened the door, as parents were often gone. The conditions were quite sad. One time I noticed a couple of the girls were not there, and I asked their friends if I should wait for them before starting. "Oh no," one said. "They won't be here. They went downtown shoplifting." It was said as casually as if they were playing ball down the street.

A few years after graduating, I began to think about citizenship. I knew I would never live in Scotland again, even though visits home were wonderful. I made inquiries and took classes in American history and citizenship, and in the summer of 1971 I attended the naturalization ceremony in Portland. It was an exhilarating experience, and as I left to walk back to work, I wanted to stop people and shout, "I'm an American!"

There was an organization in town called The Portland Americanization Council. It has since disbanded, but at that time they were celebrating their 50th anniversary. I was very surprised when I received a call from one of their leaders telling me that I had been chosen as Portland's New Citizen of the Year! I was invited to a luncheon event in downtown Portland at which they presented me with several gifts, and copies of the Declaration of Independence and the Bill of Rights. TV cameras were there and I had my Fifteen Minutes of Fame (probably more like two), as it was documented on the evening news.

The following spring, to mark the birthday of George Washington on February 22nd, the Americanization Council had a huge celebratory event at one of the local high schools. As it was their 50th Anniversary, they went all out, with the mayor, politicians, and many local dignitaries there and a full scale musical production with the high school choir, band and drama students. I was highly honored, along with the other folks who had achieved citizenship that year. I had been asked to prepare a speech, which was well received, so the whole evening was very special.

I had become active in a little store-front mission in downtown Portland. It wasn't a feeding mission, but a thriving little church that drew families from around the metro area, as well as having an outreach to the local girls and men who frequented the area. It had an active missions program, and one of my friends left to go to Kenya, to minister at a Bible School. And so it was that after about a year, I felt that God was opening the door for me to visit her. That was in the fall of 1971.

My plane landed in Nairobi around 2 o'clock in the morning. The airport was deserted, and after meeting Doris, we headed towards where she had parked. I noticed in the hall a couple of tall African men approaching from the opposite direction, smartly dressed in suits and ties. As they came nearer, I found myself staring as I thought I recognized one of them. Sure enough, it was a young man whom I had known in college through the international students group! Watson had attended Warner Pacific College, on the other side of Portland, but a small group of us had become close friends as we attended many Christian events, retreats, etc.

We enjoyed a wonderful few minutes, as we caught up on how life had led us, and how God had caused our paths to cross on the other side of the world! Watson had continued his education in Scotland, of all places! He has since become a highly-esteemed leader in the African church scene. Like cruising on what had been the Carinthia, it made me know that God was directing my steps, even in the middle of an African night.

I spent a month with Doris, helping as I could around the Bible School, and going with her out to the bush on the weekends, taking turns preaching there with a little P.A. system. Although never having met prior to that time, we enjoyed fellowship with beautiful Christian brothers and sisters. We were welcomed into homes, and enjoyed Sunday dinners in their mud huts, with chickens pecking at our feet.

It was the month of Graduation for the students, a busy time for the staff, and because of my office skills, I was able to help them out typing final tests, etc. I loved the work and was very open when some of the staff suggested that I might want to stay on, giving me some of their paper work to take care of. However, I will always appreciate the wisdom of the older lady who headed the work. "What are they doing," she asked me one day, "Trying to give you a call?" With several clear directions from the Lord, I realized that although I loved the work, it was not God's will for me to be there permanently.

After graduation, some of the missionaries took a break and rented a small house in Mombasa, on the shores of the Indian Ocean. It was very refreshing to see a different area of Kenya, and we enjoyed being able to splash around in the warm ocean waters across from our vacation home. As the week came to an end, I had to bid farewell to my new friends and start on my journey home.

As I left the Nairobi airport on the shuttle to catch my plane home, I turned around and noticed a very large red neon sign over the airport door. It read NO ENTRY. I knew God was sending me home to Portland, but Kenya will always have a special place in my heart.

Meditations

Malachi 3:10
"Bring all the tithes into the storehouse, that there may be food in My house, and try Me now in this," says the LORD of hosts, "If I will not open for you the windows of heaven and pour out for you such blessing that there will not be room enough to receive it."

This is the only place in the Bible where we are invited to test God. And my husband Bob and I have found throughout our lives that indeed God is faithful to His Word.

Shortly after I got my first job in Portland, a friend at our residence presented a different job opportunity where she worked, at a higher salary. I wanted the increased pay check. However, as I was reading in Hebrews 13 I came across the phrase in verse 5: "be content with such things as you have." As a brand new-born Christian, I felt this was the Lord telling me to stay where I was. This was the first time I got an answer from the Scriptures, but it was only the first of many occasions, especially in my early years as a Christian.

I have also found that what we plan often turns out to be what HE planned, and we get to enjoy surprises, like the "who'd have thought it" meeting with Watson. When we give our day over to the Lord in the morning, asking Him to guide our steps He will lead us, not just for our own enjoyment but to be used by Him. Sometimes it can be a chance meeting with a stranger in a grocery store, or a prayer for someone in our retirement community.

CHAPTER 14

He who Findeth a Wife

GOD'S PROVIDENTIAL DIRECTIONS proved delightful shortly after I returned to Portland. In our little church, there was a new fellow on the platform playing guitar with our minimalist band. I thought he looked interesting! However, when the worship was over, he came down and went and sat with—his wife!! Oh well!! I became friends with Bob and Laura and enjoyed their company at mission events. But within about a year, Laura, who had been suffering with Lou Gehrig's disease, passed away. Long story short, Bob and I started seeing each other, and we were later married in that same little mission.

Although he had worked for many years at a Portland dairy co-op, Bob also had a small farm about 18 miles out of town. When he and I were courting, one of his cows gave birth to a beautiful little calf whose picture I had to capture on my camera. I sent one of these snapshots to my folks, who immediately responded by return mail, "Forget about the calf—send us a picture of Bob!!" At that point they had no idea what their future son-in-law looked like!

I made my wedding dress on an ancient treadle sewing machine that I had picked up at a barn sale at a local farm. It was a Singer machine, but it had obviously seen better days, having been used as a stepping stool to reach stuff on high shelves in the barn, and as a place to store old paint cans. But I took it home and scraped off the years of neglect and refinished it. My dress turned out quite nicely, even if it wasn't the quality of the one I copied in a designer shop!

The mission was packed with our friends and family, and we enjoyed our honeymoon driving around Oregon, from the coast, down south, and then to Central Oregon.

Our first year of marriage was my first experience of farm life, and I loved it. We had a small orchard, and since I was not working, I had ample opportunity to can dozens of quarts of fruit from our own property. We had plums, pears, cherries and apples galore, as well as u-pick peaches from local farmers. And I enjoyed spending time just being around the cows we had, throwing them apples over the fence.

Our home was small, and had undergone a couple of remodeling jobs before my time there. What had originally been the garage had become the living room, which is unremarkable except for one thing. Our 120-foot-deep well had been located in the garage. So it had become part of our living room, and resembled a fireplace, with closed doors in front! We always had wonderful water that passed every test with flying colors when we sold.

When we were married, I also acquired two adult (twin) children, Lonnie and Connie, grandchildren Laura and Billy, and later TWIN great-grandchildren Kaitlyn and Valerie. We are not close geographically, but we can burn up the phone lines chatting with them! We enjoy holidays together, and our sweet great-granddaughters are high school graduates working in the retail business. We've also vacationed with them, camping in central Oregon. The kids are all very much into the outdoor scene, and whatever the season (deer, elk, etc.) they are usually out in the wilds.

A couple of years after our wedding, we decided to make a trip back to Scotland so everyone could meet Bob and he could see where I got my start. My parents were elderly by that time, but we had no idea how providential that trip was. During the three weeks we were there, Daddy at 85 went from excited host to frail and failing. We had only been back in Oregon a few weeks when we got word that he had passed from this life.

That was one of the most difficult times of my life. I was torn between wanting to go home for the funeral, but realized there was nothing I could do to alleviate the sorrow everyone was feeling. Broken-hearted, I spent a couple of days of indecision before going into our bedroom and throwing myself across the bed sobbing. I needed an answer quickly, and I knew only God could give it to me.

And He did, through obscure scriptures in Jeremiah 16:5 and 15:19 "Do not enter the house of mourning, nor go to lament or bemoan them" and "Let them return to you, but you must not return to them." It was in my daily reading—I wasn't looking for sad scriptures. But I knew instantly I had my answer, and from then on I had great peace while mourning from afar.

At that time I had no idea what the ramifications of the whole scripture meant, but in just two months my mother "returned to us." She decided to travel 6000 miles and come to Portland to be with us, her first trip to the west coast. It was a very healing time for all of us, besides giving her space to be away from her now lonely home. And within the next year, she made two more trips to Portland, one with my oldest sister Isabel. It was well known in the family that Mum's favorite shop was the travel agency, and she was never happier than when she had a plane ticket in her purse!

On these trips, she and I had wonderful chats about life. I asked her if they were unhappy with the news when they found out she was pregnant with her sixth child. "Oh never!" she replied. "Daddy and I were always thrilled when there was another baby on the way!" Daddy was 47 when I came along.

In another of our quiet heart-to-heart talks, Mum asked me what I thought it meant to be a real Christian and to be ready to meet Jesus. I told her as simply as I could that you must respond to Jesus' call to come to Him, ask Him to come in and take control of your life, forgive your sins and prepare you to meet Him. As we talked, she looked at me with an honest and open heart and said, "I've done those things." It gave us both great peace to have the most important decision in life confirmed in just a few moments and we sealed it with a hug.

But our time together wasn't always somber. We laughed as Mum sang, complete with a prop from our garden, "Only a Faded Rose," a sad dirge about sweethearts parting during the sinking of The Empress of Ireland! What made it funny was that it was the song she chose when asked to sing (at age 15) at a friend's wedding! Fortunately, the bride saw the funny side of it, and they laughed whenever they met years later.

Bob and I did go back to Scotland on vacation two years later. And just five years after Daddy, Mum joined him in Heaven. She had been a cancer survivor for twenty years, but it eventually cost her life. I have no doubt that she and Daddy are enjoying their heavenly life together. Not long after Mum's death, it was very comforting to me that Isabel came out to Portland to be with us for a few weeks. I really appreciated that visit.

Shortly after we were married, Bob and I sold our farm home and moved closer into town, still about ten miles from city center. That in itself was an adventure, because after living on a farm, every city lot we considered looked very restricting. However again the Lord led us to a home that suited us to a T. The property adjoined a small pasture with two Shetland ponies! The neighbors were Swiss dairy farmers who had herds of cattle on a nearby hill. God really does know the desires of our hearts!

The neighborhood had lots of young families with small children, and since I was not working, I began praying about having Bible clubs in our home. So for about the next ten years we had children in our home, hearing the Gospel about how Jesus loved them so much. I didn't make a huge issue out of things like healing, but we did take prayer requests and prayed for their childlike desires. Things like "My Grandma has a sore knee" were prayed over in faith. One little 5-year-old boy couldn't have candy because he was diabetic. But a few months later he was eating them with everyone else. "Oh he doesn't have diabetes anymore," his sister told us, "so he can have candy." The children could earn points by bringing their Bibles, learning a memory verse, etc. At the end of the school year, the points could be used at day camps, or for other prizes.

My very favorite incident of all the years of Bible clubs, involved two little girls whose mom would drop them off and sign "I love you" in sign language. They were shy about telling me that their parents were deaf. But one day, Gladys (about 10 years old) came running to the door and couldn't wait to tell me "what God told me!" Since the place was buzzing with kids waiting to start, I told her to save it until after class. So the minute the club ended, she came running up, "Can I tell you now what God told me?" "Of course!" I said.

She related to me that she was standing in their bathroom fixing her hair and she HEARD God say to her "I love you"! She was so earnest, I knew she wasn't lying or making it up. "He told me two times that He loved me!" It still brings tears to my eyes. God knew that child couldn't hear her mommy or daddy tell her they loved her, so in His immense love, He made sure she knew HE loved her!

Bob was very much part of the clubs also. When he was home, it wasn't unusual for them to come to the door and ask, "Can Mr. Beaman come out and play?" He always loved little kids, and loved to roughhouse with them.

It's now been well over forty years since I threw those apples to the cows. But how do you record years and years of daily living, of sharing life with the one you love? God has been so faithful to us, has taken us to about twenty nations, all but two states and every Canadian province west of Quebec.

We've had a close call with a tornado in Oklahoma, survived a horrendous early summer snow storm in Montana, and yodeled and sung together in gatherings in living rooms and small churches both in Scotland and here in the U.S. We've had four dogs, lived in three different homes, and now are enjoying life in a beautiful retirement community.

We've also had vacations back to Scotland, and have spent time around St. Andrews. Although we're not golfers, we had fun walking around the Old Course, and did some putting on their putting green. There's an authentic bottle dungeon in the Castle, and St. Andrews University, the oldest in Scotland, counts both Prince William and Kate as alumni; and a martyr's monument honors early Christians who were burned at the stake. The ancient church has an original King James Bible among their other valuables. And it's fun to walk along the West Sands and have the wind make havoc of your hair! Can you tell we love St. Andrews?

Family updates:
My brother, Tommy, and his family returned to Scotland after just a couple of years in Canada. Sadly he was killed in 1986 when he was crushed by some industrial equipment. Isabel and her family lived for decades on the shores of Loch Lomond, managing an estate which had been in the hands of the Smollett family for centuries. Isabel passed away in 2009.

So now we are three. Betty, who has lived her entire life within a mile of Glenfender, is living in a retirement home in Clydebank. Tommy's daughter, Margaret, who went as a toddler to Canada in 1956, is now Betty's wonderful companion, taking very good care of her elderly aunt. Shortly after 9-11, after more than 70 years, Betty decided to visit the U.S. Her plane was delayed for some time; after all, what was an old Scottish lady with a thick accent doing with a brand new British passport that said her birthplace was Charlotte, North Carolina! A couple of years later she was planning another trip, but didn't want the fuss. So she went to the US Consulate in Edinburgh. I got a phone call from her: "Guess what! I'm now an American citizen!" So on later trips she carried both passports!

Jessie lives in a senior apartment in Belleville, Ontario, with her four children scattered from Vancouver to Dubai. Her oldest daughter is administrator on an oil rig off the coast of Nova Scotia. Last Christmas, a letter from her second daughter included a picture taken at Buckingham Palace, where her husband was awarded an MBE. The Queen was indisposed but Prince William chatted with them for a few minutes. Jessie's two sons are in business in British Columbia and Ontario.

When we were considering selling our home and moving to a retirement residence I was faced with something that bothered me. In the dining room there were several walkers lined up against the wall. Back in our home, I mused "God, I don't know if I'm ready for this—living with walkers around." In an instant I heard His response. "It isn't always about you!" I knew exactly how Gladys had felt when the Lord spoke to her.

And so here we are, enjoying our retirement and growing closer each day to our Lord. He continues to lead us, and has given us many opportunities to pray for residents about their health issues. As He told me, it isn't always about us or what we think we want. But true contentment comes from being where HE wants us, helping where we can, and walking dogs as needed!

As you meditate on my story and adventures in life, I hope you will find that your life has been just as exciting, and certainly worthy of passing on to your children and grandchildren. And may you find the Lord Jesus to be your all-sufficient One.

Meditations

My husband has always been for me the biggest blessing the Lord has given me. For well over forty years, we have been a team on this road called Life. I like to think that although we never consciously planned it, our married life has mirrored, in a way, the way we were both raised. Bob's parents also had a very strong marriage, rooted in the hard life of a rancher. And although one was rural and the other suburban, our family backgrounds were very similar -- hard working, God-fearing, and based on mutual respect, with a heaping tablespoon of humor along the way.

I often think about the children I had in Bible clubs. I wonder where they are now, what they're doing, and if they've found their way with the Lord. I'm encouraged by the teaching of the Lord about the seeds we sow. The seed is the Word of God, and when it is sown, it does just what earthly seeds do. If it is watered and tended with prayer, it produces after its kind.

The following verses have been very meaningful to me and I trust will help you also.

Isaiah 12:2, 5
Behold, God is my salvation, I will trust and not be afraid; For YAH, the LORD, is my strength and song; He also has become my salvation... Sing to the LORD, for He has done excellent things; This is known in all the earth.

Joshua 22:5   But take careful heed...to love the LORD your God, to walk in all His ways, to keep His commandments, to hold fast to Him, and to serve Him with all your heart, and with all your soul. .

Ruth 1:16   (Sung at our wedding)
Entreat me not to leave you, or to turn back from following after you; for wherever you go, I will go; and wherever you lodge, I will lodge; Your people shall be my people, and your God, my God.

Philippians 1:6
Being confident of this very thing, that He who has begun a good work in you will complete it until the day of Jesus Christ.

Colossians 1:10 (my life verse)
(That I) may walk worthy of the Lord, fully pleasing Him, being fruitful in every good work, and increasing in the knowledge of God.

Hebrews 12:2
Looking unto Jesus, the author and finisher of our faith, who for the joy that was set before Him endured the cross, despising the shame, and has sat down at the right hand of the throne of God.

Share your thoughts:
Dbeaman1@comcast.net
Or c/o Living Hope
PO Box 7400
Aloha, OR 97007

Made in the USA
San Bernardino, CA
31 May 2016